THREE PLAYS
FELICITY BROWNE

Felicity Browne

THREE PLAYS

THE FAMILY DANCE
ODDS ON OBLIVION
THE GREAT AUNTS

OBERON BOOKS
LONDON

First published in this collection in 2004 by Oberon Books Ltd
521 Caledonian Road, London N7 9RH
Tel: 020 7607 3637 / Fax: 020 7607 3629
e-mail: oberon.books@btinternet.com
www.oberonbooks.com

The Family Dance first published in 1976 by Samuel French

A catalogue record for this book is available from the British
Library.

ISBN: 1 84002 521 2

Contents

THE FAMILY DANCE

CAST

BEN MUSGRAVE
TOBY MUSGRAVE, his brother
DIANA VERNEY, his sister
SOPHIE MUSGRAVE, his wife
VICTORIA MUSGRAVE, Toby's wife
MICHAEL VERNEY, Diana's husband
CHARLES VERNEY, Diana's brother-in-law

TIME: 1976
PLACE: The kitchen of the Musgraves' house.

Act 1: Early Evening
Act 2: Later the same evening

The Family Dance was first performed at the Criterion Theatre, London, on 5 June 1976, with the following cast:

BEN MUSGRAVE, Alec McCowen

TOBY MUSGRAVE, Michael Bryant

DIANA VERNEY, Helen Lindsay

SOPHIE MUSGRAVE, Annette Crosbie

VICTORIA MUSGRAVE, Judy Parfitt

MICHAEL VERNEY, Anthony Nash

CHARLES VERNEY, James Warwick

Directed by Jonathan Hales

Designed by Eileen Diss

ACT I

A vast kitchen. Early evening.

The ceiling is lost in darkness. There is an enormous deal table, covered with loaded plates; a large Aga cooker where the range once was; a towering dresser covered with plates and objects, with drawers underneath. Copper preserving-pans, etc, are hung on the wall. Various bits of non-kitchen furniture – tables, a piano, etc, have been stacked up in a corner, but the kitchen is so large they make little impression. A door leads to the rest of the house, another to the garden. An opening leads to the pantry.

As the CURTAIN rises voices are heard off, then a crash.

BEN: (*Off.*) That is *enough!*

TOBY: (*Off.*) Diana said –

BEN: (*Off, cutting in.*) Never mind.

TOBY: (*Off.*) But the sideboard –

BEN: (*Off.*) I'm not moving anything else. (*Pause. In surprise.*) There's Socrates. Who put Socrates here? (*Silence.*) What's he doing here? (*Silence.*) Oh, the whole house is upside down. Here. Give me a hand –

TOBY: (*Off.*) What with?

BEN: (*Off.*) Socrates, of course.

TOBY: (*Off.*) Thought you weren't –

BEN: (*Off, cutting in.*) Shut up! Take that end.

TOBY: (*Off.*) You're going to –

BEN: (*Off.*) Who – ow!

TOBY: (*Entering.*) – scrape your knuckles.

(*BEN and TOBY enter from the house, staggering under an enormous rocking-horse. BEN MUSGRAVE is a square, powerful, volcanic figure, given to sudden outbursts. He puts far too much energy into everything, and looks as if he may burst out of his clothes. His hair is wild. He is aged about forty-five, and wears a dinner-jacket. TOBY, his brother, is thin, looks pale, ill and gone to seed. He is elegant and,*

11

unlike BEN, looks good in his clothes. He is fortyish and neat in his movements. He also is wearing a dinner-jacket. BEN puts his end down carefully, then examines his knuckles with passion, licking them.)

BEN: Why didn't you say so?

TOBY: I just did.

BEN: Blood poisoning – (*He goes to the sink to wash his hands.*)

TOBY: From a wall?

BEN: They're out of their minds.

TOBY: Who?

BEN: Diana and Sophie. (*He explodes.*) Don't they realize what sort of a week I've had? Don't they realize I need a rest to give me strength for Monday? (*Pause.*) But what do I find? The house is to be packed with young people. (*The sunset fades.*)

TOBY: Your idea entirely.

BEN: Young bloody people.

TOBY: 'Let's all band together and give a dance for the children's friends.' You said.

BEN: Why do they have to be young here?

TOBY: One of your expansive days.

BEN: Isn't Berkshire full of houses to be young in? Other people's houses?

TOBY: *You* wanted five hundred guests. *You* –

BEN: (*Turning on him.*) Well? Isn't that what the house is for? Why do you think I keep on this blasted back-breaking millstone of a house, if it is not so that our-children-may-dance-in the rooms where their forebears danced?

TOBY: Bit of an anachronism, some might say.

BEN: Anachronism? A vast pile like this where brothers and sisters and their husbands and wives and children co-exist in the warm, crowded atmosphere of a working-class slum? It's not an anachronism, it's dodoland.

TOBY: All I was saying was that it's no use complaining about the guests when you invited them yourself. One hundred and fifty of them.

BEN: What a good idea.

TOBY: But with refusals and chickenpox we're down to a paltry one hundred and twenty-five.

BEN: I hope they're grateful. They – who's got chickenpox?

TOBY: All invited by you, so for once you cannot blame –

BEN: I'm not having them here with chickenpox –

TOBY: – anyone else.

BEN: – I might get it. Does no-one in this house consider me?

TOBY: Those with chickenpox won't come.

BEN: How do you know?

TOBY: They're in bed.

BEN: No-one with spots is to cross the threshold. I forbid it. Examine them at the front door.

TOBY: How about acne?

BEN: Acne?

TOBY: Endemic in that age group.

BEN: (*Jumping on Socrates and riding him furiously.*) No-one considers me. My health. My well-being. My – happiness – are – of – no concern – to anyone – in this house. To hell with them. All. All. All.

TOBY: (*Laughing excitedly while BEN rides.*) Do you remember playing Greenmantle?

(*BEN slows down and stops entirely. He sits very still.*)

BEN: Greenmantle! 'There is a dry wind blowing through the East, and the parched grasses await the spark. And the wind is blowing towards the Indian border. Whence comes that wind, think you?'

TOBY: (*Very quietly.*) 'Where would you start the fire?'

BEN: (*Very quietly.*) 'Where the fuel is driest.'

TOBY: (*Very quietly.*) 'Sister Anne, Sister Anne, do you see anybody coming?'

BEN: (*Suddenly starting to propel Socrates, shouting.*) Holy War! Holy War! Jehad! Jehad!

TOBY: (*Seizing a chair and riding it backwards as if for chair-polo, shouting.*) Peter's got through. The Russians are round the flank. The town is burning. Glory to God, we've won, we've won!

BEN: The Cossacks! The Cossacks! God! How they're taking that slope! By Heaven, we'll ride with them! With them!

TOBY: Oh, well done our side!

BEN: Ride knee to knee for the city!

TOBY: Ride for Erzerum!

TOBY / BEN: (*Shouting together.*) Erzeru-u-um!
(*Socrates goes slower and slower, and finally stops.*)

BEN: A good ride. That was a good ride.

TOBY: You were ten. I was five. You were confined to barracks – the nursery – for disobedience. You wanted to go ratting with Gammel. You were furious – white and dangerous – as you rode for Erzerum. (*Pause.*) You were always the most exciting person in the world.

BEN: Me? My dear Toby, take another look. (*Silence.*) I don't expect you've looked for years. There's nothing much left. (*Pause. He rides thoughtfully backwards and forwards.*) Was it worth it? Was any of it worth it?

TOBY: Was what what?

BEN: Oh – giving up my life – of which I had considerable hopes – to support this everlasting maw of a household. Are we happy?

TOBY: Happy.

BEN: I thought we would be, you see. I thought that if, in a mad, shifting, intolerable world, we could all stay united in this house, then our children would have roots, and having been brought up together would support each other through life –
(*TOBY buckets along on his chair.*)

BEN: – and I thought we would all contribute. But here's the rub. No-one, except me, works. And the burden of supporting this household is making me old and frantic. *You've* never had a job –

TOBY: I'm waiting –

BEN: Waiting?

TOBY: (*Rising from the chair.*) Erzerum – Erzerum.

BEN: Look, I'm serious. Then Diana – well, Diana marries
a man who won't work –

TOBY: Michael's all right.

BEN: Of course he's all right living off the fat of the land at
my expense –

TOBY: He keeps Diana happy.

BEN: (*Ironically.*) Oh good. And what about me? Who keeps
me happy?

TOBY: Neither of us qualifies for married bliss.

BEN: Victoria and you –

TOBY: Yes.

BEN: Not the world's best marriage. Is it?

TOBY: Hardly.

BEN: What –?

TOBY: I don't know. (*Pause.*) Being unhappily married takes
up such a lot of the day.

BEN: And night.

TOBY: And night.

BEN: Can't you – ?

TOBY: Leave it, Ben.

BEN: Why don't you – ?

TOBY: Leave it.

BEN: But surely you –

TOBY: Leave it. Leave it. Leave it.

BEN: (*Dismounting from the horse.*) Oh Socrates, Socrates,
what an ugly world. Only you are unchanged. How
superb you look. Your nostrils are as red as ever, you
look so young. (*Pause.*) I'm old, Socrates. Old and frantic.

TOBY: (*Lifting covers and inspecting dishes.*) They'll never eat
all this.

BEN: Don't touch those plates.

TOBY: What will happen to their livers? (*Pause.*) Why not?

BEN: Because Diana will blame me.

TOBY: She's only our sister –

BEN: The young don't have livers. They're slim and
     beautiful. They and Socrates.
TOBY: You scared? Of Diana?
BEN: Of course not.
TOBY: I *am* surprised. Frightened of Diana. You.
BEN: I don't like being blamed unfairly.
TOBY: I'll own up.
BEN: I shall still be blamed.
TOBY: Why?
BEN: Because I'm the oldest. The responsible one.
TOBY: Hardly relevant.
BEN: Of course it's relevant.
TOBY: When you were five times as old as I was, yes.
     When you were twice as old, yes. But now? You're forty-
     five. I'm forty.
BEN: It may not matter outside this house. But here – if
     you touch that ham – it's my fault.
TOBY: Oh, fiddle faddle, fiddle faddle. (*He strokes the horse's
     mane.*)
BEN: And stop pulling Socrates' mane.
TOBY: The rights of primogeniture don't extend to
     Socrates. He's as much mine and Diana's as yours.
     (*Pause.*)
BEN: I'm afraid that's nonsense. Socrates belongs to me.
TOBY: Why?
BEN: He always has. He's mine, that's why.
TOBY: Ours.
BEN: Mine.
     (*Pause.*)
TOBY: Ours.
     (*DIANA VERNEY, their sister, enters front the house. She is
     in her early forties, built on a large scale, big head, big nose,
     big body, big feet, but very handsome. She has a loud, firm,
     not unattractive voice, an excellent carriage and considerable
     grace. She is dressed in splendid, conventional evening dress,
     bare-shouldered, and looks grand, terrific, beautiful and self
     confident. No nonsense.*)

DIANA: You're doing nothing – what are you thinking of?

TOBY: I say –

DIANA: Do you imagine we're ready? (*She takes a necklace from the dresser and puts it on.*)

TOBY: Your best – once-a-year dress –

DIANA: That there's nothing to be done?

TOBY: – Balenciaga –

BEN: – for an evening at the sink.

TOBY: Haven't you overdone it?

DIANA: (*Taking an apron from a hook and putting it on.*) How could I overdo it for the children's friends? Who could matter more?

(*TOBY bows to her. She curtsies.*)

Jane has toothache. Where are Sophie and Victoria? Why aren't they here? I can't bear it if her evening is ruined by toothache – I've given her salt and hot water – where *are* Sophie and Victoria?

TOBY: Haven't seen them.

DIANA: Well, why *not,* they're your wives. You all knew I had to go out all afternoon visiting Aunt Lalage, but it hasn't occurred to any of you to do anything helpful, and we're not nearly ready –

TOBY: If it comes to that, where's your husband?

DIANA: Michael? He's in bed –

BEN: (*Moving to go.*) What an extraordinarily good idea and how stupid of me not to have thought of it myself. Luckily it's not too late.

DIANA: (*Taking silver and two cloths out of a drawer.*) Don't be silly, he's got 'flu. I told you before, but you never listen.

BEN: (*Exploding.*) How am I to keep alive in a house seething with 'flu, acne, and chickenpox?

DIANA: Go to bed, indeed. We've only you and Toby left to dance with anyone who's left out.

BEN: There's Charles.

DIANA: Charles won't help if it doesn't amuse him.

TOBY: Which it won't –

DIANA: (*Giving TOBY some spoons and two cloths.*) Here,
Toby, take these and give them a polish – we need every
bit in the house.

BEN: Am I to house not only my sister's husband, but my
sister's husband's brother –

DIANA: He *is* your brother-in-law.

BEN: He is not, he is not! He's *your* brother-in-law.
(*TOBY puts one cloth in BEN's pocket.*)

DIANA: – and families are the most important things in the
world.

BEN: To me he is my brother-in-law's brother, not a
relationship where the majority would consider
hospitality necessary –

DIANA: I've powdered Grizelda's spots – they hardly show.
Did you move the sideboard?

BEN: – but if I have to house him he can pull his weight
and dance his legs off.

DIANA: The sideboard. (*She brings two lettuces from the
pantry.*)

BEN: I've had enough of Charles, He makes trouble –

TOBY: Leave it, Ben.
(*Pause.*)

BEN: Why –

TOBY: Leave it.

DIANA: Can't you polish a bit quicker?

BEN: And who does Socrates belong to?

DIANA: You can't leave the sideboard where it is.

BEN: Tell Toby, will you?

DIANA: It takes up too much space, everyone will bump
into it.

BEN: Tell Toby.

DIANA: Tell him what?

BEN: Who – Socrates – belongs to.

DIANA: Toby, of course.

BEN: Nonsense.

DIANA: Don't be silly. He was a present from Toby's
godfather.

BEN: Socrates was here before Toby was born.

DIANA: Months before. Mother was very upset in case Toby was stillborn.

TOBY: Stillborn? Why should I be stillborn?

BEN: But he's mine –

TOBY: Never had any intention of being stillborn. (*Pause.*) I can see it would have solved a lot of problems. Shaving – marriage – whether to go to the movies or stay at home –

BEN: He's always been mine.

TOBY: – not to mention disease, old age, and death. (*Pause.*)

BEN: (*Business-like.*) How much will you take for him? (*Pause.*)

TOBY: He's not for sale.

DIANA: (*Snatching the polishing-cloth from TOBY in a fury.*) Neither of you has any sense – don't you realize the time? The guests will be here –

BEN: Why not?

TOBY: You can offer me nothing I want.

BEN: You're short of money.

TOBY: Yes.

BEN: In ever-increasing difficulties.

TOBY: Yes.

BEN: Sell him.

TOBY: No.

BEN: Swop.

TOBY: What for? Mess of pottage?

BEN: I'm serious.

TOBY: Dust and ashes?

BEN: What do you want?

TOBY: Thirty pieces of silver? Cloud-capped towers? Gorgeous palaces?

BEN: You've been drinking. Already.

TOBY: The great globe itself? Or all the rights of primogeniture? (*Pause.*) No.

DIANA: Oh, stop it, I'm ashamed of you both.

BEN: But it's very important.

DIANA: To whom?

BEN: Me. Of course.

DIANA: This is the children's evening. Not yours. They're going to remember this evening for the rest of their lives. Tonight they're going to make memories to warm their old age. Turn yourself outward, Ben. Think of them. And remember Sophie. (*She rummages in drawers and begins counting forks.*) Look at these forks – Victoria promised to clean them.

BEN: Sophie?

DIANA: Sophie.

BEN: Oh yes, Sophie.

DIANA: You must know your wife's name after seventeen years.

BEN: What's the matter with Sophie?

DIANA: Nothing. Until you upset her.

BEN: Why should I?

DIANA: Because you always do. Eleven – twelve – She's perfectly all right during the week – useless about the house, of course, but quite happy. And then on Friday night you come back. Seventeen – eighteen – And then you do it. Every time. As you come through the door. If only she could shout back at you like the rest of us – Oh bother, Ben, you've made me lose count, how selfish you are. What are you doing, both of you? Nothing – nothing. Toby, get the candlesticks out.

TOBY: Where are they?

DIANA: (*Indicating.*) In that cupboard.
(*TOBY runs to the cupboard and looks.*)
She could shout back at you, you know. She's not frightened. Or weak.

TOBY: They're not here.

DIANA: Of course they are, why can't you look?

BEN: She preserves her energy. For her painting. None of it comes my way. A mere husband.

TOBY: (*finding the candlesticks and bringing them to the table.*)
Here they are. Well done, Toby. I say, Diana, they're
here. Look, here they are, I found them.

BEN: Oh, stop chirruping.

TOBY: Why should she waste her energy on a monster?

BEN: A monster?

TOBY: 'If you look upon monsters, take care you do not
become one yourself; for, should you gaze down into the
abyss, the abyss may enter into you.'

BEN: (*Struck.*) That's good.

TOBY: Thank you. (*He sits and polishes.*)

DIANA: I wish you'd both be quiet –

BEN: Your own?

TOBY: Nietzsche.

DIANA: How can I count these forks?

BEN: I like it. Say it again.

TOBY: If you look –

DIANA: No – no. *No.*

BEN: Something the matter?

DIANA: She ought to leave you, really. I shall tell her so, I
think.

BEN: *What?*

DIANA: Not now, of course. I'll have a little talk with her
tomorrow.
(*Silence.*)

BEN: I support this household.

DIANA: Michael –

BEN: Yes, Michael contributes – but his books – what was
the last one, *Golfing Tales of an Old Codger,* butter few
parsnips.

TOBY: A rare phrase.

BEN: I support this household. Slave for it – for all of you.
I pay for every bloody thing – yes, I know Michael pays
the subscription to *Country Life,* but I don't read it.

TOBY: Only I don't know what it means.

BEN: Everything I pay for. Gin – roof repairs – cat food.
And what do I get in return?

TOBY: Thanks.

BEN: Thanks? *Thanks?* You're out of your mind.

TOBY: Praise.

BEN: That's what a normal household would give for benefits received. But *you?* While I shorten my life with overwork, what happens? What happens, I ask you?

DIANA: (*Bridling.*) His books may not make much money but they get very good reviews.

BEN: I will tell you what happens.

TOBY: Gratitude.

BEN: My wife escapes if I come near her. My little brother turns the household into a public spectacle by getting indecently drunk – at my expense, naturally – in the middle of the afternoon on the village street – you thought I didn't know, you're mad, people flocked to tell me as I got off the train. Meanwhile, back at the happy home, my sister, whom I trusted, wants to persuade my wife to leave me –

DIANA: I don't expect to succeed.

BEN: I should hope not. She knows which side her bread is buttered on – (*Glaring at TOBY.*) – and so, may I say, do you.

TOBY: Gratitude. (*Pause.*) And love.

(*Silence.*)

BEN: I didn't mean it. (*With passion.*) I didn't mean it, I didn't mean it.

(*SOPHIE, BEN's wife, enters from the house. She is in her late thirties, fairish, thin and slight, dressed in paint-bespattered jeans and carrying a sketch-book and pencil. She often tries to sink into the background to avoid the noise of family life roaring round her; but her face is neither weak nor humble, and when she notices anything that interests her, light and life pour into it. All her attraction comes from these sudden glimpses of interior life. Unlike her husband and sisters-in-law she is both quiet and still. Her movements when she is out of her element – ie doing any kind of kitchen job – are awkward. DIANA would peel ten potatoes in the time SOPHIE would take to peel one.*)

DIANA: Toby, why are you sitting down? You haven't finished –

TOBY: No?

DIANA: The coasters, look, they're filthy – and the candlesticks, you haven't done them, they're disgusting – (*She sees SOPHIE.*) Good heavens, Sophie, don't you realize guests will be coming? What are you doing dressed like that?

SOPHIE: (*Looking down at herself, surprised.*) I was working, I forgot.

DIANA: Working?

SOPHIE: Painting.

DIANA: Oh, I thought you meant *working,* like the rest of us.

SOPHIE: I'm sorry. I forgot.

DIANA: Forgot? Forgot the children's dance? I can't understand you, Sophie –

SOPHIE: Something went right. It doesn't often. I didn't want to stop halfway.

DIANA: Then you didn't forget.

SOPHIE: I suppose not. No. I didn't. But I'm here now. What would you like me to do?

DIANA: Where's my list? Ah. Do you think you can do salad dressing?

SOPHIE: Of course.

DIANA: You ought really to be changing –

SOPHIE: It takes me five minutes.

(*SOPHIE goes off to the pantry.*)

DIANA: That's much better, Toby. Even Thwaites couldn't have polished them better.

TOBY: Well done, Toby, we knew you had it in you –

DIANA: Ben, I did ask you to move the sideboard.

(*SOPHIE enters with a tray on which are oil, vinegar, a pepper-mill and a basin, which she puts on the table, and sets to work.*)

BEN: You did, indeed.

DIANA: But it's still there.

BEN: I struck.

TOBY: (*Moving to the door.*) Come on, Ben.

BEN: Toady.

(*BEN and TOBY exit to the house.*)

DIANA: What are you doing, Sophie?

SOPHIE: The salad dressing. Like you said.

DIANA: But where's the lemon?

SOPHIE: Lemon?

DIANA: We always use lemon in the salad dressing.

SOPHIE: Oh. I didn't know.

DIANA: But we *always* use lemon. How could you not know?

SOPHIE: I suppose I didn't notice.

DIANA: (*Going to the pantry.*) I wish you'd try not to be so dreamy. (*She returns with a lemon and a squeezer.*) Really, it makes me cross. How long have you been in this house?

SOPHIE: Seventeen years.

DIANA: There. (*She gives her the lemon and squeezer.*) Married to Ben for seventeen years. And you still haven't noticed that in *this* house we have lemon in the salad dressing. Oh Sophie, how *can* you not have noticed? How *can* you be so thoughtless?

SOPHIE: It's not intentional –

DIANA: I never said it was, but it's very upsetting for everyone. I don't know why you do it.

SOPHIE: I said. It's not intentional.

DIANA: You don't try. (*Pause.*) Sometimes I think you don't notice any of us.

SOPHIE: (*Stung.*) Indeed I do. Look. (*She opens her sketchbook and shoves it under DIANA's nose, turning the pages.*) Look at that.

DIANA: Why, it's Victoria in one of her moods – when she can't get what she wants.

SOPHIE: And that –

DIANA: Nicola running towards you – oh, that's really very amusing, it's *her*.

SOPHIE: And that –

DIANA: That's – oh no. Ben's not like that. You've made him so – threatening. And – looming. Why, you've made him into a monster, you know. How very odd that you should see him like that. (*Pause.*) After all, he is your husband. Now put it away. Everyone will be arriving and nothing's ready. And do you know what Victoria's doing?

SOPHIE: No.

DIANA: I'm *telling* you. She's playing billiards with Charles. Now, of all times.
(*BEN and TOBY enter. TOBY goes to pour a drink.*
SOPHIE sits and mixes the dressing.)

BEN: Another vertebra gone.

DIANA: Well done, Ben, that's very nice. Now what next – ?
(*She looks at her list.*) Yes. Toby, come with me and look *very* carefully to see nothing breakable has been left lying about. You too, Ben –

BEN: No, it's rest hour.

DIANA: Then you can at least do something useful.
(*She throws the polishing-cloth at him.*
DIANA and TOBY exit to the house.
Silence.)

SOPHIE: (*Mumbling, head down over the dressing.*) Had a good week?

BEN: What?

SOPHIE: (*More clearly.*) I said, 'Had a good week?'

BEN: (*Polishing forks.*) I've been in the house for twenty-four hours. Why ask now?

SOPHIE: Suppose we haven't seen each other much.

BEN: When I came to bed you were asleep. When I woke up you'd gone. And I haven't seen you all day.

SOPHIE: I've been painting.

BEN: No doubt. But you can hardly blame me if we 'haven't seen each other much'.

SOPHIE: I didn't –

BEN: I'm sorry. I thought you did.

(*Silence.*

They speak together)

BEN: It never occurs to Diana that I need a rest at the weekend.

SOPHIE: The children are very excited.

(*They both stop.*)

SOPHIE: Sorry.

BEN: Go on.

SOPHIE: No, you go on.

BEN: What did you say?

SOPHIE: Oh, nothing –

BEN: You did. You said something.

SOPHIE: Nothing important. What did *you* say?

BEN: Look, I asked you what *you* said.

(*Pause.*)

SOPHIE: I said, 'The children are very excited'. About the dance. (*Pause.*) What did you say?

BEN: (*Slowly.*) I said, 'It never occurs to Diana that I need a rest at the weekend'. (*He rises.*)

(*Pause.*)

SOPHIE: Oh.

BEN: So neither of us said anything. (*He cuts a slice of bread.*)

SOPHIE: Don't you think it's time we did?

(*BEN puts the bread in the toaster.*)

Ben, I want a divorce.

BEN: (*Not listening.*) No-one cares, of course, but I haven't had my tea.

SOPHIE: Ben –

BEN: (*Rummaging in a cupboard for jam.*) What is it?

SOPHIE: I want a divorce.

BEN: A divorce? Who from?

SOPHIE: You, of course.

BEN: Me? Don't be absurd. Of course you can't have a divorce. (*He brings the jam to the table.*) What utter nonsense. Divorce me? What for, for heaven's sake? I'm

the easiest man in the world to live with. *Divorce.* Good
grief. We've been married for fifteen years.
(*Smoke begins to rise from the toaster.*)
SOPHIE: Seventeen. Seventeen years.
BEN: Seventeen, then. Seventeen years. Well, you might as
well stick it out to the end after seventeen years. (*He sits.*)
Do you know, I'm absolutely shocked. No, really, the
more I think of it. And hurt. By God I'm hurt. I must
say, Sophie, I'm very surprised, I –
(*Smoke pours from the toaster.*)
(*Rising.*) You bloody fool, you've burnt my toast – (*He
throws the burnt toast into the sink.*)
SOPHIE: The thing's broken.
BEN: Everything's bloody broken, oh, all the love in this
house is flying out of the window.
SOPHIE: I mean it, Ben.
BEN: You break every bugger I buy – don't give them the
slightest love and attention – of course they break.
SOPHIE: You might just as well let me go.
BEN: Your average toaster needs affection. Encouragement.
Understanding.
SOPHIE: We could both get a bit of peace.
BEN: (*Viciously.*) But you haven't any of that, have you?
SOPHIE: Any of what?
BEN: Affection. Encouragement. Under-bloody-standing.
(*He picks up the jam pot.*)
SOPHIE: You must see we'd be far better apart.
BEN: (*Conversationally, eating a spoonful of jam from the pot.*)
Frightfully good jam.
SOPHIE: We'd both be so much happier –
BEN: I suppose you didn't make it.
SOPHIE: – saner –
BEN: Bought at enormous cost from some blasted
supermarket.
SOPHIE: – have more chance of surviving –

BEN: (*Putting the jam down.*) Divorce. Good God, what are you thinking about? Don't you realize marriage is for life? What about your vows?

SOPHIE: Vows consistently broken carry little weight. (*Pause.*)

BEN: What are you on about?

SOPHIE: Who were you talking to on the telephone this morning? (*Pause.*)

BEN: The garage. (*Pause.*)

SOPHIE: The garage.

BEN: The garage.

SOPHIE: I heard you, Ben. I heard what you said. (*Pause.*) Look, I don't know who she is and I don't really care –

BEN: (*Shouting.*) Why not? Why don't you care? How dare you not care? (*More quietly.*) Listening round corners. (*Shouting again.*) It's intolerable the lack of trust in this house. Life's not worth living without trust.

SOPHIE: That's what I'm saying. So let me go.

BEN: Look. It's all right. I forgive you.

SOPHIE: Let me go.

BEN: I forgive you. (*Pause.*) In any case I don't see why you should mind. Sex is hardly your strong point. You've never liked it –

SOPHIE: I get so tired –

BEN: – wanted it –

SOPHIE: – and then you get so cross.

BEN: – wanted me. (*Silence.*)

SOPHIE: You know I bore you.

BEN: You never *listen* to me – if only you'd listen –

SOPHIE: I do listen.

BEN: When I tell you which marmalade – which coffee – I like –

SOPHIE: Oh – that.

BEN: *That! That!* Are my tastes so irrelevant? My needs –
my desires –

SOPHIE: But I'm not good at –

BEN: – listening. *Listening!*

SOPHIE: I do listen. But you shout so – I have to protect
myself.

BEN: What from?

SOPHIE: Noise. I don't know. I don't know.

BEN: Am I so awful? So repulsive?

SOPHIE: It's not – oh, sometimes it's almost all right.

BEN: What is?

SOPHIE: Us. Sometimes. When we both try – like that
picnic last month.

BEN: Great day that was.

SOPHIE: We both enjoyed it.

BEN: But I got stung by a wasp.

SOPHIE: Then, of course, you screamed and yelled and it
was over.

BEN: Well, it hurt.

SOPHIE: So we went home.

BEN: Anyhow, the grass was damp.

SOPHIE: But before –

BEN: Before?

SOPHIE: Before you were stung –

BEN: What about it?

SOPHIE: We were close.

(*Pause.*)

BEN: Yes.

SOPHIE: Why?

BEN: We're married, aren't we? Why shouldn't we be?

SOPHIE: In that case, why aren't we more often? Oh, can't
we learn?

BEN: It's not a question of learning. All you have to do is
relax and – *listen*. Not escape into a private world and
shut me out. (*He looks in the refrigerator and takes out a
bowl.*) Ah, mulberries. (*He goes to the table with the bowl.*) I

think of you – when I first saw you. Skating. You looked so full of promise. Hopeful.

SOPHIE: I liked skating.

BEN: (*Furiously.*) I wanted you. I've always wanted you. But I've never got you.

SOPHIE: We've had children.

BEN: What holds you back? I can make other women melt. Why not you? Why? Why? Why? Why did you look so happy when you were skating? So full of life? It was a lie. *Why* don't you want *me*? Why don't you want me? (*He shakes her.*)

SOPHIE: (*After a pause.*) I've never felt like that about anyone.

BEN: *Skating!* (*Pause.*) These mulberries have got mould.

SOPHIE: That's not mould.

BEN: Of course it is.

SOPHIE: No.

BEN: Look at it.

SOPHIE: Yes, I know, but –

BEN: I know mould when I see it.

SOPHIE: No, it's duck stock.

(*Silence.*)

BEN: What?

SOPHIE: It's duck stock.

BEN: Duck?

SOPHIE: I splashed it on to the mulberries. When I was putting it in the fridge.

BEN: Duck stock.

SOPHIE: I was helping Diana. I got most of it off.

BEN: Most of it.

SOPHIE: There's only one or two globules left –

BEN: Globules.

SOPHIE: – and they don't taste at all, because I've tried.

(*BEN pours the mulberries into the waste-bin.*)

BEN: No-one – no mulberry fancier – will say thank you for mulberries and fatty duck stock.

SOPHIE: You only had to scoop it off. (*Pause.*) And now you're cross.

BEN: I'm not cross. Not at all. Just disappointed. I like mulberries. I was looking forward to them. (*Pause.*) Just – disappointed. I suppose mulberries and fatty duck sauce was suggested by one of your frightful women's magazines. The Common Market touch, how to make your average Austrian at home.

SOPHIE: Austria isn't in the Common Market.

BEN: If you try serving it up to the French you'll be in trouble.

SOPHIE: I've *told* you how it happened –

BEN: If you imagine your average Frog is going to be gratified at a mixture of that nature, you're mistaken.

SOPHIE: – but, as usual, you don't listen.

BEN: It may be *Haute Cuisine* to you –

SOPHIE: You just go on shouting –

BEN: – but to them it's frankly *merde.*

SOPHIE: – and shouting and *shouting* –

BEN: Because you never *listen.* You never think about me. You burn my toast –

SOPHIE: (*Screaming.*) Oh, get a new toaster.

(*Pause.*)

BEN: Why?

(*Pause. SOPHIE takes hold of herself.*)

SOPHIE: New ones – are quicker. Better. Faster.

BEN: You think new ones are more electric. You imagine this one works partly by candlepower –

SOPHIE: (*Slowly.*) Oh, how silly you can make me sound.

BEN: – and it's the candles that cause the smoke.

SOPHIE: How *silly.*

(*Silence. They look at each other.*)

Couldn't *you* leave *me?* Me and the children? (*Pause.*) In peace.

BEN: (*Amazed.*) Don't be silly. I live here.

(*DIANA enters from the house.*)

Diana, talk to Sophie – she's out of her mind. She wants a divorce. From *me*. She's off her head.

DIANA: Ben, your *tie* –

BEN: Will you *talk to her.*

DIANA: It's falling apart before the evening's begun.

BEN: Diana –

DIANA: Not now, Ben. It's the children's evening. You mustn't be selfish. Now come along and help Toby and me. And Sophie, go and change. It takes you more than five minutes, you know. You think you're very quick but you're not – you take just as long as the rest of us. (*She takes BEN's hand and pulls him out.*) *What* a time to choose to have a nasty, selfish quarrel –

(*DIANA and BEN exit to the house.*

SOPHIE, left alone, puts her head in her hands.

VICTORIA comes in from the garden entrance, very fast. She is TOBY's wife, beautiful and very alive, tall, dark and flashing. She is self-willed and strong-minded; not a comfortable or easy person to have around; not particularly nice but with generous moments and sometimes appreciative. She can turn a room black at the drop of a hat if things do not go exactly as she wants them to. She is sudden and graceful of movement; and beautifully dressed.)

VICTORIA: I suppose she found the silver. (*Getting out cleaning things.*) Hell. Of course she did. 'Victoria promised to do it – and look – look' – What's the matter with you?

SOPHIE: I've just asked Ben for a divorce.

VICTORIA: (*Interested, but not stopping work.*) Why now? (*She sits at the table to polish forks.*)

SOPHIE: What do you mean?

VICTORIA: Not worse, is it? Than it's ever been?

SOPHIE: Yes. I'm more – frantic.

VICTORIA: What an evening to choose. What did Diana say?

SOPHIE: Just that.

VICTORIA: And Ben?

SOPHIE: Brushed it aside.

VICTORIA: Of course. (*Pause.*) You'll never get him to listen, you know. You can't win.

SOPHIE: I must –

VICTORIA: How can you? You've never been able to fight Ben. What makes you think you can begin now? After all those years?

SOPHIE: I must. I'm swamped.

VICTORIA: He'll walk over you. Like he always does.

SOPHIE: If I can't get out I shall die.

VICTORIA: He won't oppose you. He won't hear. It's not worth trying.

SOPHIE: I must.

VICTORIA: (*After a pause.*) You're not going to anyone else, are you? (*She cleans the silver rapidly and noisily, not looking up.*)

SOPHIE: Only to myself. Back to myself.

VICTORIA: Is it worth it? Why upset things?

SOPHIE: I've told you. Because I shall die if I don't get away.

VICTORIA: *Die?* Don't be absurd. (*Her eye is caught by the sketch on the table. With an exclamation of fury.*) Why do you always draw me looking like that?

SOPHIE: Like what?

VICTORIA: Like – like *that.*

SOPHIE: (*Gazing at the drawing, lost in thought, forgetting VICTORIA.*) Is it too – implacable? (*Pause.*) The single-minded pursuit of self-interest –

VICTORIA: (*Outraged.*) Sophie!

SOPHIE: (*Coming to.*) I'm sorry, I'm *really* sorry, I didn't mean anything, it was just an – an aspect of you that interested me – Oh, please don't quarrel, I couldn't stand it with Diana's dance looming over us –

VICTORIA: *Diana's* dance – whose house is this?

SOPHIE: Ben's.

VICTORIA: Who is Ben's wife?

SOPHIE: Oh, I know, but –

VICTORIA: It's *your* dance – your house – why is everything always Diana's?

SOPHIE: The house belongs to Diana because she fills it. It's hers by natural right. (*Exclaiming.*) Of course it's not *my* house, when even the noise of family life exhausts me.

VICTORIA: Noise? What noise?

SOPHIE: Oh, the thundering clash of ego bouncing off ego. And no-one in this house ever talks. They all roar and yell –

VICTORIA: I'd never noticed. Do they? We?

SOPHIE: All I want – all I ever hope for – is time for work and then to get through the day quietly. No trouble. No noise.

VICTORIA: A modest wish.

SOPHIE: But seldom, if ever, realized.
(*DIANA enters from the house, running.*)

DIANA: (*To VICTORIA.*) You haven't cleaned –

VICTORIA: I have. I have! Look! Glowing! (*She holds bits up.*)

DIANA: Well, you hadn't done it twenty minutes ago.

VICTORIA: Ah, but I have now.

DIANA: Yes, but you shouldn't leave things until the last minute.

VICTORIA: Why not?

DIANA: It's a mistake, that's why. Sophie, you haven't changed yet.

SOPHIE: (*Rising.*) Oh – I'll go and do it now.
(*SOPHIE, muttering, exits to the house.*)

VICTORIA: (*To DIANA.*) How grand you look – lacking only long white gloves – (*She rises.*)

DIANA: (*Perfectly seriously.*) No, I've got them. Of course.

VICTORIA: I *don't* believe it. (*She puts the cloth away.*)

DIANA: (*Producing the gloves.*) Of course I have. Full evening dress means long white gloves.

VICTORIA: Meant. In the days of the Romans.

DIANA: Romans?

VICTORIA: Oh, don't you remember the Romans? Who ruled our childhood and straightened our backs? The nannies, oh and the great-aunts, what great-aunts there used to be. But they're a long time gone, taking with them their long white gloves, and their cucumber sandwiches – their croquet mallets, their leather-bound prayer-books, their –

DIANA: I'm sure it's very clever, Victoria, but I don't know what you're talking about.

VICTORIA: You don't find it at all odd dressing up with long white gloves to pass an evening washing-up in the kitchen? Because that's what we'll be doing.

DIANA: It's the *principle.*

VICTORIA: Wouldn't jeans and an apron be more in keeping?

DIANA: Of course not. We're having a dance.

VICTORIA: The *children* are having a dance – we're doing the washing-up – fetching and carrying. We ought to be dressed as maids, flunkeys – (*Pause.*) You're not listening.

DIANA: Victoria, could you stop Toby drinking? Just for this evening?

VICTORIA: How?

DIANA: Well, talk to him. (*She puts the salad dressing on the refrigerator.*)

VICTORIA: What good will that do?

DIANA: You're his wife. You ought to be able to stop him – it's absurd that you can't put your foot down.

VICTORIA: Toby would agree with everything I said. Then he'd go off and drink the same as usual. So why waste breath?

DIANA: If you weren't so careful with your breath Toby might be happier – you don't give him enough love, that's the trouble.

(*SOPHIE enters wearing a Jean Muir dress.*)

I don't think you try very hard. (*She examines SOPHIE.*) There you are, Sophie. You're rather – covered up, aren't you? I mean, it's a very nice dress, but no-one would guess you had a good figure, really you're quite *hidden*. And the colour is somehow – the same colour as the rest of you.

VICTORIA: Sophie isn't beige. (*The colour must depend on the available dress – but the word describing it should be evocative, funny or strange.*)

DIANA: Don't be silly, Victoria, of course she isn't. But her hair's pale and her face is pale and so is her dress. Perhaps if we pinned a rose on her –

VICTORIA: No.

DIANA: Yes, look – I'll just find a pin. (*She rummages in a drawer.*)

VICTORIA: No. It's wrong.

DIANA: It will make all the difference.

VICTORIA: It will look macabre.

DIANA: Macabre, really, Victoria –

SOPHIE: Oh, can't you both stop shouting over me?

VICTORIA: Shouting?

DIANA: Don't be silly, we're helping you. You don't want to look drab, do you? (*Shutting the drawer, and sighting the carving-knife.*) Who on earth put the carving-knife here?

SOPHIE: I did.

DIANA: But it's the wrong place. *This* is where the carving-knife goes. (*She moves it. Pause.*) Fancy you not knowing that.

VICTORIA: The carving-knife belongs wherever Sophie puts it. It's *her* house. Not yours. Not mine. Hers.

SOPHIE: Oh, please –

DIANA: Of course, Victoria. We all know that. But there's still a right and wrong place for a carving-knife. The right place is here. In this drawer. Ah. Here's a pin. (*She pins a rose on SOPHIE.*) There. (*Pause.*) Oh dear, it doesn't – Never mind, it's better. (*Pause.*) I *think* it's better. (*Pause.*) Perhaps a belt – No. Well, never mind, dear, you have such nice eyes. Now – I must go and receive the guests.

VICTORIA: (*Emphatically.*) That's Sophie's place.

SOPHIE: (*Quietly but intensely.*) Oh Victoria, please, *please.*
(*BEN enters from the house.*)
BEN: (*To SOPHIE.*) Why are you wearing that rose?
(*DIANA seizes BEN and makes him waltz.*)
It looks dreadful.
DIANA: Oh Ben, how silly you are.
BEN: Diana, tell her to take it off.
(*SOPHIE exits to the house.*
As BEN and DIANA dance round the room they duck
whenever they reach a certain spot.)
Why was Sophie wearing that appalling rose? That dress
needs nothing – it's marvellous. (*Duck.*)
DIANA: *Marvellous?*
VICTORIA: You're ducking.
BEN: Of course. Hadn't you noticed?
DIANA: But it's so drab.
BEN: My dear Diana, you don't know *anything.* (*Duck.*)
VICTORIA: Why are you ducking?
DIANA: I gave her the rose. I thought the dress needed
cheering up.
BEN: Cheering up? Diana, you're unbelievable. (*Duck.*)
VICTORIA: What – are – you – ducking – for?
DIANA: (*To VICTORIA, plonking.*) To avoid the hams, of
course.
VICTORIA: What hams? There aren't any hams.
BEN: A dreadful, blowzy rose –
DIANA: (*Plonking.*) No, but there used to be.
BEN: – in the middle of that perfect dress –
VICTORIA: How many years ago?
DIANA: Years ago?
VICTORIA: Since there were hams? Really, this house is
absurd – don't you realize? The shibboleths – no-one
must sit in this chair because Annie died in it –
DIANA: Don't be silly, Victoria. *That's* the chair Annie died
in.
VICTORIA: Then this is the one James used to rest his
gouty foot on, so that's sacred too.

DIANA: I hope you're not being funny about poor James. He suffered a great deal.

VICTORIA: In every corner of the house there's a private god.

BEN: (*Sitting down.*) I'm not enjoying myself. What is Sophie on about?

VICTORIA: She wants to leave you.

BEN: *Why?*

VICTORIA: For peace. Quiet. Time to work.

BEN: But she *can't* want to leave me – not seriously. Why?
(*TOBY enters from the house.*)

VICTORIA: Perhaps it's no fun.

BEN: Fun! How silly. How frivolous. I'm going to bring her to her senses. And she can begin by taking that rose off.
(*BEN exits to the house.*)

DIANA: (*Going after him.*) Leave her *alone,* Ben. Leave her *alone.*
(*DIANA exits.*
Silence. VICTORIA starts washing lettuces.)

TOBY: Well. Here we are. In a room together. Alone.
(*Silence.*) A rare occurrence. Happening seldom by day.
Never by night. As you like it, I suppose. As you like it.

VICTORIA: A great year for slugs.

TOBY: If only I could fancy someone else. Ideal solution.
But from the moment I saw you you filled my heart and my mind and my eyes, and will do until my last breath.
(*Silence.*)
'If any beauty I desired and got.
'Twas but a dream of thee.'
Do you remember how happy we set out to be? In another world.
(*Silence.*)

VICTORIA: The aphids, too, are doing well.

TOBY: If you would only tell me in what way I – displease you, perhaps I could do something about it. (*Silence.*) No.
I've frozen you up just by talking about it. Let's put it away again. (*He opens a drawer.*) There, creepy-crawly, In

you go. (*He slams the drawer shut.*) And stay there. (*Pause.*)
How right you are to find talking a bore. A mouth
opening and shutting. What's the use, you say. And how
right you are. As always. Always right, my wife. (*Pause.
Briskly.*) Well now, what's left? (*He pours himself a whisky.*)

VICTORIA: Do you really want another whisky?

TOBY: Do I want another whisky? Do I want another
whisky? Well, do you know, I rather think I do. (*Pause.*)
Do you mind?

VICTORIA: It's nothing to me.

TOBY: Yes, I know.

VICTORIA: For the sake of the children you might try and
stay sober –

TOBY: Ah! The children's dance!

VICTORIA: – just for once.

TOBY: Supposing we were to meet this evening for the first
time – no past –

VICTORIA: I imagine they would prefer it.

TOBY: – I would have a fresh start with you –

VICTORIA: Although I expect they're so used to it that it's
a matter of indifference to them –

TOBY: – and, I suppose, fail again.

VICTORIA: – as it is to me.
(*Silence.*)

TOBY: Some of those children – now fresh, unscarred – will
meet their Waterloo on that dance floor tonight. As I did
when I first saw you.

VICTORIA: (*Ironically.*) You wish to call off the dance.

TOBY: (*After a pause, quietly.*) Yes. I do wish to call off the
dance. But it's in motion. Unstoppable. (*He shivers.*) But
who wouldn't call it off, call it all off, if he could?

VICTORIA: Anyone willing to accept a few scars.

TOBY: My marks and scars I carry with me. My sword I
give – No. Nothing to do with me. I have not lived
bravely. I have ducked at the sight of trouble and legged
it from the field of battle. At the sound of the trumpet I
have buried my head beneath my pillow. (*Pause.*) I can

feel you sneering. But you were born brave. What merit is there in that? (*Silence.*) With you, speech is superfluous.

(*DIANA enters from the house.*)

Victoria is growing bored at the thought of the guests –

VICTORIA: (*Without interest.*) Toby, you're behaving like a fool.

TOBY: – and so am I. We've all heard too much about them. Let's call the whole thing off.

DIANA: (*To VICTORIA.*) Can't you stop him drinking? Just for this evening?

VICTORIA: (*As a statement.*) How can I.

TOBY: You may address me, you know. I am here. (*Looking in the glass.*) 'Among those present was debonair Toby Musgrave.' (*Pause.*) In hell.

(*DIANA picks up the coasters and candlesticks. She speaks to VICTORIA hurriedly and quietly, but TOBY overhears.*)

DIANA: Why don't you do something? Why do you care so little?

TOBY: (*Pouring another drink.*) Just what I always say myself. (*Pause.*) You realize we're not a stable enough household to have a children's dance? There are too many echoes, undertones, overtones. The guests will be embarrassed and want to go home.

DIANA: Toby, I hope you're not going to get the horrors again tonight. It's very upsetting for the rest of us. (*She goes to the door.*) Do you hear, Toby? No horrors.

(*DIANA exits, and VICTORIA follows.*)

BEN: (*Off.*) Nothing to do with me is important, we all know that. First thing we learn in this house.

SOPHIE: (*Off, exhausted.*) I've said I'm sorry. You'd better take this one as well, Ben. I just forgot.

(*TOBY takes another whisky, and holds the glass to Socrates' mouth.*

BEN enters with some letters.)

BEN: (*As he enters.*) Leave me alone. Leave me alone. Stop
following me about. Under her bloody paintings. My
whole week's post.

TOBY: Socrates was thirsty. (*Pause.*)

BEN: Why won't you sell him?

TOBY: Don't want to.

(*Pause.*)

BEN: Why?

TOBY: Don't care. (*He does a drunken dance to the tune of 'I
Won't Dance'.*)

'Why should I?

I don't care.

How could I?

I won't care.

Merci beaucoup.'

BEN: No sense in being flippant.

TOBY: No sense in being serious. No sense. No sense
anywhere.

BEN: Rubbish.

TOBY: Oho. You think sense is about somewhere, do you?
Where? Where? Lurking in the subterranean corners of
the mind? Come out of there, sense, we know you're in
there.

BEN: Oh, don't be ridiculous.

TOBY: Aha. You think it's in the world about us. Outside.
Exterior to the mind. But where? Under the table,
perhaps. (*He gets down on all fours and crawls under the
table.*) Nothing there. Only a half-chewed bone.
(*Pause. He reappears with the bone.*) Wonder if it's mine. I
hope not. Let me see. (*He sits on the floor and takes off his
shoes and socks, beginning to count his toes.*)

BEN: You're drunk. Again.

TOBY: Drunk or sober, my dear chap, I've got to make sure
I'm all there.

BEN: Oh, pull yourself together.

TOBY: Be reasonable, Ben, I can hardly do that before I
know whether there's any of me missing. (*He goes back to*

his toes.) Eight, nine, ten. All present and correct. Spectacles, testicles, wallet and watch. (*Feeling himself, and getting it in the wrong order.*) No, no. Spectacles, testicles, wallet and watch. (*He gets it right.*) Yes. Right.

BEN: Do get up.

TOBY: (*Rising.*) I wonder whose bone that was? One of the guests, perhaps. We must watch out for someone dancing a toe short. (*He mimes a man dancing in agony minus a toe.*) (*The telephone rings. TOBY dances through the door to answer it in the passage.*) (*On the phone.*) Hullo – No. None of us is here. I haven't seen any of us for days. Can't remember when I last saw us. (*He slams the receiver down.*)

BEN: I suppose you realize that might have been for me? That it might have been important? The way you behave is *intolerable.*

TOBY: *My* behaviour intolerable, good grief, what about you? Filling the house with people whose bones drop off.

BEN: (*Opening his letters.*) This should have been answered days ago.

TOBY: Furthermore, when they've dropped off do they tidy them away? Call for a dustpan and brush? Not your guests. Just leave them lying about under the kitchen table, where anyone might fall over them, and where they constitute, no doubt, a considerable health hazard. Litter louts. That's the class of person you ask to the house. (*He goes to the door, staggering rather, opens it, and goes out, shouting at the top of his voice.*) KEEP BRITAIN TIDY!

(*TOBY is immediately pushed back into the room by DIANA, who enters and shuts the door hastily.*

Just before the door closes there is a loud noise of guests arriving.)

DIANA: Oh, Toby, you *must not*, not this evening. (*She goes to the sink and washes some watercress.*)

(*BEN sits and reads his letters.*)

TOBY: Now don't sidetrack me. I was helping Ben – who
has his troubles like the rest of us – to look for sense.
He's lost it and I was helping him. Fraternal solidarity.
I'd tried under the table –

DIANA: (*Taking napkins off various dishes, garnishing the ham
with the water-cress, etc.*) Don't be silly, Toby. You know
perfectly well you won't find sense lying about under the
table.

TOBY: Aha. *I* know that. Of course. You know it. But Ben
doesn't. We've just got to ease him along. (*He sings.*)
"Ease him along,
Singing a song,
Side by side."
(*He tiptoes over to BEN and bellows in his ear.*) I'm with
you, Ben!

BEN: (*Leaping up furiously.*) Get out! Get out of my house.

DIANA: Don't be silly, Ben. He's your brother.

BEN: Other people don't support their brothers. Other
people's brothers grow up.

DIANA: That's not the point.

BEN: What *is* the point? He gives me no pleasure. I don't
enjoy having him around. I ought to get rid of the lot of
you.

TOBY: Ah. That's what I say. Get rid of the lot.

BEN: Do you think I wanted to spend my life like this?

TOBY: Get the decorators in.

BEN: I'm fed up with the life I lead in this house. I pay for
everything. All the burden falls on me. Money goes like
water – and what do I get in return?

DIANA: I always think it's such a pity you're a stockbroker.

BEN: (*Unable to believe his ears.*) Didn't you hear what I said?

DIANA: (*Placidly.*) Yes, Ben, of course. (*Pause.*) I just think
it's such a pity you're a stockbroker.
(*BEN collapses.*)
And I do wish you wouldn't talk about money all the
time. You know we weren't allowed to mention it when
Mother was alive, and now you never stop. She'd be very

shocked, you know. Really I don't know what she'd say. (*Briskly.*) In any case, you're being very silly because you know you couldn't do without us.

BEN: Oh, couldn't I?

DIANA: You? Do without the children?

BEN: Don't talk to me about the children. They've been screaming about the house all day. I haven't had a moment's peace – my eardrums are at risk.

DIANA: What a pity you've grown so old –

BEN: They've been behaving –

DIANA: – in a childish manner. Like children. At the thought of a dance their hearts have risen. They don't know what's coming, but they expect everything – every unknown pleasure in the world. (*She glares at BEN. Pause.*) How childish of their hearts to rise so lightly. In a childish manner, sillily.

(*Silence. BEN kisses her hand.*)

TOBY: (*Climbing up on the dresser and opening a cupboard above it.*) The difference the decorators would make in this house; they'd throw everything away – everything. Look – Jacobean candle snuffers – snuff – snuff – snuff. We even have an elephant gun, though I haven't seen many elephants lately – not in Berkshire – not at large. Look at all this junk. Look –

DIANA: What?

(*TOBY pulls out a 1930s portable wireless from the cupboard. They all gaze at it.*)

Good heavens. Nanny's old portable.

TOBY: You see? *Nothing* in this house gets thrown away.

DIANA: Things often come in handy.

TOBY: 'Monday Night at Eight.'

DIANA: Oh! The week's high spot.

TOBY: When Nanny used to bring her portable into the night nursery –

DIANA: – if we'd been good all week.

TOBY: She used to stretch it, though. She was decent –
Always a helping hand from Nanny. (*Pause.*) Why isn't
she still around?
(*BEN gives an exclamation of disgust, TOBY jumps down
and puts the radio on the table.*)
It's all very well for you to sneer. She could always cope
with everything I couldn't learn – tying my shoes –
dressing – keeping me tidy. If only, instead of being
spent on useless expensive schools, the money had gone
on providing me with a first-rate Nanny on a life
contract. Now come along, Master Toby, there's a good
boy. Will you have another whisky if Nanny pours it for
you? There it goes – down the little red lane.'

BEN: I cannot believe that all I deserve from life is to have
Toby infesting my house, wearing my clothes, drinking
my drink, and drooling on about Nanny.

TOBY: (*Singing affectedly.*) 'It's Monday night at eight
o'clock.
Oh, can't you hear the chimes.
They're telling you to take an easy chair.
And settle by your fireside.
Look at your *Radio Times*.
For Monday Night at Eight is on the air.'

DIANA: Oh, do you remember the game? Nanny was keen
on that.

TOBY: 'Guess what, guess why, guess the who and how.
Of the things we'll ask you now –
Get your pencils and your paper out.
You're the winner if you know about.
Who the what the where the why and when.
Which and wherefore and how now,
Which and wherefore and how.'

BEN: You've carried that inane drivel in your mind for over
thirty years. How I'd hate to see the inside of your head.

TOBY: *Who* is Ben? *What* does he want? *When* did he turn
sour? *Wherefore* is he desperate? *What does he want?*
(*Silence.*)

BEN: You can't play that game, little brother. You haven't got the courage. Or the energy.
(*Pause.*)

TOBY: No. You're right. (*He pours himself another whisky.*) Everyone in this house is right. Except me. Take my wife. Never stops being right. And Diana. Always at it. Even Ben has an occasional stab at it. Rightness is all.
(*CHARLES enters from the house. He is MICHAEL's brother, amusing, lightweight, stylish, an easy talker, very social. He is much younger than his brother, and is wearing a dinner-jacket.*
Before CHARLES shuts the door loud music is heard.)

CHARLES: Michael's shouting for you.

DIANA: Oh, I promised to take his temperature.
(*DIANA rushes out.*)

BEN: (*Shouting after her.*) Can't he even lift a thermometer?

TOBY: The dance floor red in tooth and claw, where those who have are given abundantly more, and those who have not lose even that which they had.

BEN: (*To TOBY.*) If you've got a memory like that, why don't you do something useful with it? Get a job?
(*CHARLES laughs.*)
(*Menacingly.*) Yes? Did something amuse you? Something about my brother, perhaps?

CHARLES: Always good for a laugh, you and Toby, to a simple outsider like myself.
(*Pause.*)

BEN: Outsider.

TOBY: You're being too modest. You play quite a role in our lives. Wouldn't you say so, Ben?

BEN: Considerable.

TOBY: Our brother-in-law's brother – almost a relation.

BEN: A figure on the periphery of family life.

TOBY: Oh, closer in, closer in.

BEN: You're right.

TOBY: Periphery means edge.

BEN: An ill-chosen word.

TOBY: Yes. Nearer home than that, isn't he?

CHARLES: That will do.

BEN: Much nearer.

TOBY: Close?

BEN: Very close.

TOBY: In a position of trust and affection?

CHARLES: I said that will do.

BEN: That's right.

TOBY: Trust.

CHARLES: I'm not going to spoil Diana's evening by
      having a fight with you two.

BEN: Fight? My dear fellow, you know how we love having
      you here – proud to have you in the family.

TOBY: We consider you an asset.

BEN: And then, you make such a difference to Victoria.

TOBY: Victoria. My wife.

CHARLES: Rotten games you two play.

BEN: He says we play rotten games. I wonder what he
      means?

TOBY: Too clever for me.

BEN: Our games rotten – what about yours? Cuckoo in the
      nest – that's your game.

CHARLES: If it weren't for Diana –

BEN: You'd do what?

CHARLES: (*To BEN.*) I'd knock your head off. (*To TOBY.*)
      Both your heads.

BEN: (*Savagely.*) Adding physical assault to treachery.

TOBY: I *said* we shouldn't have a children's party.

CHARLES: (*To BEN.*) So shut up.

TOBY: Poor little perishers.

BEN: You're in no position to tell me to shut up.

TOBY: Headless hosts.

CHARLES: I'm telling you all the same – whatever my
      position.
      (*CHARLES goes out, furious.*
      The music is heard, wilder, until he shuts the door.)

TOBY: Areas of treachery and counter-treachery are best left unexplored.

BEN: Rubbish.

TOBY: What do you gain?

BEN: My feelings are relieved.

TOBY: (*Pouring himself a glass of water.*) Let's just leave it lying quietly. I don't wish to lose what little I still have of my wife.

BEN: How can you be so feeble – ?

TOBY: A little is better than nothing.

BEN: Is it?

TOBY: I console myself.

BEN: With whisky.

TOBY: Well, that. But I say to myself either – you don't get what you want, or you get it. But when you do, it's probably too late. In either case, there's nothing you can do. So why worry?

BEN: But you used to have hopes.

(*DIANA enters.*
Music is heard.)

DIANA: Did we really ask as many as that? There seem to be hundreds of them. What a lovely noise they're making, and it's hardly started. Now, Ben, you take one of the heavy trays – I've got the children lined up to take everything from you.

BEN: Come on, Toby. (*He picks up a tray.*)

DIANA: Remember, no children in the kitchen.

(*BEN exits.*)

(*Calling after him.*) No children in the kitchen!

BEN: (*Off.*) NO CHILDREN IN THE KITCHEN!

DIANA: Tell them to put everything with the rest of the food in the dining-room. Sophie! Victoria! Come and help.

(*TOBY picks up a tray.*)

Charles! No, Toby, not that one, you're not very steady on your feet, you know.

(*TOBY puts the tray down and picks up a plate of ham.*

BEN enters, followed by SOPHIE and VICTORIA.)

BEN: They're all covered in spots.

DIANA: Ah, Sophie, you take the duck, and see that the napkins are on the table, will you, dear? There you are, Victoria, you take the pudding trolley and tell the children not to put the puddings on the table, they'll make marks.

(SOPHIE exits with the duck, VICTORIA wheels off the trolley.)

Where is Charles? Why isn't he helping?

BEN: *(Shouting off.)* Charles!

DIANA: *(Calling after VICTORIA.)* Oh, and Victoria, leave the trolley in there to bring things back on. Ben, you take the chicken-and-tongue. Has Nicola put the hamster away?

BEN: I'll tell her.

(BEN exits with the dish of chicken-and-tongue.)

DIANA: *(Calling after BEN.)* He'll be trodden underfoot.

BEN: *(Off.)* Nicola, put that bloody hamster to bed. I know he's lovely, darling, but he can't dance.

(SOPHIE enters and picks up another tray of food.)

DIANA: *(To SOPHIE.)* Did Toby drop anything?

SOPHIE: No.

DIANA: Oh, good.

(SOPHIE exits. TOBY enters.)

Oh, there you are, Toby. Well done. Now you take in the bread – *carefully*, dear.

(TOBY exits with an armful of loaves, picking up his glass of whisky and the bone on the way.)

(Looking round and checking.) Rice, salad, silver – now is that really everything? *(She ticks off her list.)* Yes, yes, yes. There, the kitchen's empty again.

(TOBY enters, shutting the door.)

Oh, Toby, what marvellous times we had in here when we were children. Do you remember how lovely and noisy it was? It was all such fun.

TOBY: Everyone loved us.

DIANA: *Was* it such a golden world?

TOBY: Oh yes, yes. Don't you remember?

DIANA: I think I do. But am I exaggerating? Life isn't really like that.

TOBY: It was – it was – you can't have forgotten.

DIANA: I do remember noticing things –

TOBY: Things?

DIANA: Like Mrs Eppings telling lies.

TOBY: Lies? Mrs Eppings? How can you talk like that?

DIANA: She did, Toby.

TOBY: Nonsense – she was as honest as the day.

DIANA: She was a hypocritical old baggage who cheated Mother over the housekeeping for years – and as for James, I always think he hated the lot of us –

TOBY: Diana – stop it – stop it –

DIANA: Good heavens, Toby, whatever is it? You're shaking. (*Pause.*) What on earth does it matter now? They've all been dead for years and we're middle-aged –

TOBY: I don't believe it – I don't believe any of it.

DIANA: But it doesn't matter.

TOBY: Of course it matters.

DIANA: But they're all dead –

TOBY: They're more alive to me than anyone I meet in the street.

DIANA: (*Not listening.*) Do you remember how I used to dance on the table? After kitchen tea?

TOBY: 'The table's clear, Miss Diana – get up and give us a dance.'

DIANA: It must be thirty years since I danced on that table – thirty years – good heavens, I'm forty-two. Oh, how can I be forty-two?
(*Pause.*)

TOBY: Get up.

DIANA: Oh, don't be absurd.

TOBY: Get up.

DIANA: I can't.

TOBY: Go on.

DIANA: I can't.

TOBY: Please – come on.

(*DIANA climbs up on the table.*)

DIANA: Absurd. Oh. (*In surprise.*) Everything looks different.

TOBY: You've grown.

DIANA: Yes, of course, so I have. (*Pause. She points at spaces round the table.*) That was Annie's place – James – Mrs Eppings, Mrs Eppings, let me see, who sat next to Mrs Eppings?

TOBY: Thwaites. Of course.

DIANA: Of course. Then – Jenny – Martha – (*Pause.*) – oh, Toby, isn't it empty? It's so quiet –

(*TOBY goes to the piano and starts to play a jig.*)

TOBY: Of course it's nonsense. About Mrs Eppings and James. But I wish you hadn't said it.

DIANA: (*Listening to the music.*) Oh – that jig – what's it called?

TOBY: *Rory O'More.* Of course.

DIANA: Of *course*. Annie's favourite. But there's no-one to stamp, and no-one to shout – no-one to tell me I'm pretty –

TOBY: Dance to their memory.

(*DIANA begins to dance.*
BEN bursts in while DIANA is dancing.
There is a discordant noise from outside before he shuts the door.)

BEN: Are you mad? Good grief, you weigh a ton, get down before you break the table.

(*TOBY plays a dissonant chord.*)

(*To TOBY.*) What are you looking at me like that for?

(*Pause. DIANA gets down from the table.*)

Who has to buy a new table when Two-Ton Tessie has fragmented it? She's no slip of a girl.

TOBY: She was. For a moment.

DIANA: (*Pushing past BEN.*) He's quite right, Toby. I was being childish.

(*DIANA exits.*)

BEN: (*Gazing at the door.*) What was that about? (*Pause.*)
Have I done something awful?

TOBY: How can you care so little? (*He leaves the piano.*)

BEN: But I do care.

TOBY: Then why don't you *look?*

BEN: What have I done?

TOBY: Just for a moment – Diana was light of heart. Like
she used to be. You put the years back on –

BEN: Oh God –

TOBY: – and added some.

BEN: Why didn't you warn me?

TOBY: Why didn't you look?

BEN: (*Roaring and bellowing.*) Hell! (*He moves to the stove and
fills a sauce-pan with hot water from the kettle on the Aga.*)

TOBY: What are you doing?

BEN: Boiling myself an egg. Food is the only answer to the
strain of life in this house. I want – a boiled egg.
(*He settles at the table with bread and knife and cuts thin
strips of bread with great concentration.*
TOBY also settles at the table and watches him. Silence.)

TOBY: Bread and butter fingers. (*Silence.*) You should butter
the bread before you cut it. (*Silence.*) Everyone knows
that. (*Silence.*) And you're cutting it too thin. It'll break
when you dip it. (*He picks up a bit of the bread and waves
it.*) Poor, weak, wobbly thing. Pathetic.
(*BEN glares at him, and begins tearing off thick strips of
bread with his fingers.*)
Tearing the loaf apart. What would Nanny say?
(*The water boils. BEN puts an egg in the saucepan and looks
carefully at his watch.*
SOPHIE enters.)

SOPHIE: Would you like me to do that?

BEN: You? And have it turn out like my egg this morning?
What am I saying – 'this morning'? Every bloody
morning. All I ask is a fresh egg lightly boiled. So that
when I dip my bread and butter fingers –

(*TOBY snorts.*)

Did you say something?

TOBY: No.

BEN: (*Glaring at him.*) Where was I?

TOBY: Dipping your bread and butter fingers into your lightly boiled egg.

BEN: Ah. There's the crux. They stub their toe on it. (*He goes to the dresser for salt and pepper.*) Why? Because the bloody thing is solid. Iron hard every time. (*Pause.*) Now you may think, 'What is he making a fuss about? All he has to do is mention in passing to his loving wife that he likes his egg boiled for four-and-a-half minutes precisely, and Bob's your bleeding uncle – a perfect egg every time.' But how wrong you would be. I have told my wife on an average of twice a week for the last seventeen years, and she never gets the bugger right. Seventeen years of spoilt eggs. (*He takes a plate, puts a hunk of bread on it, and then some butter.*)

TOBY: (*Going for another drink.*) But you keep on at her, don't you? At her, at her, at her.

BEN: (*To SOPHIE.*) Just for once I am going to have an egg which is a pleasure to eat. So I am cooking it myself.

SOPHIE: I hope you enjoy it.

BEN: And do you know why you are incapable of cooking me a decent egg? Because you are not prepared to give a moment's thought to my needs, fears, tastes or desires. I might as well be in China for all you care. You're not prepared to do *anything*. You won't cook, you won't make a bed and neither will you lie in it. Look at you now – you're not listening, you're not *listening*. What are you looking at?

SOPHIE: I was looking –

BEN: Yes?

SOPHIE: – at that bread.

BEN: Aha! The bread.

SOPHIE: Who tore it into chunks?

BEN: Ah!

SOPHIE: Not that it matters.

BEN: Oh, but it does. You find it disgusting.

SOPHIE: I said it doesn't matter.

BEN: You wish to begin at the other end. With a knife.
Cutting delicate, even artistic slices. Ha. (*Menacing her.*)
But what is going to happen when we meet in the
middle? Eh, Mrs Musgrave?
(*SOPHIE stands facing him.*)
Had you thought of that? (*Pause. He pulls off a chunk of
bread and hands it to her.*) Look. Have some with me. It's
an eat-in, baby, a love-in. I have a mouthful. You have a
mouthful. It's what it's all about. Bread. It's always been
like that. Two people breaking bread together.
(*SOPHIE stands there.*)
Oh, hell! (*He hurls the loaf on the floor, scattering the pieces,
then suddenly remembers and looks at his watch.*) You bloody
fool, you've spoilt my egg *again!* (*He burns himself as he
takes out the egg.*) Ooow!
(*BEN gathers the whole lot on a tray and rushes out, leaving
the door open.
Loud music and laughter are heard until TOBY shuts the
door. Then absolute silence.*)

TOBY: Drink?
(*Pause.*)

SOPHIE: What?

TOBY: Have a drink.

SOPHIE: No. (*Hurriedly.*) Why won't he let me go?

TOBY: Whisky? Have a whisky.

SOPHIE: It's just as awful for him.

TOBY: (*Pouring a whisky.*) Do have a whisky.

SOPHIE: But he can't let me go.

TOBY: *I'm* going to have one.

SOPHIE: And I can't get away – can't get away anywhere.
No refuge. No peace.

TOBY: Come and watch the children. We'll have a dance.

SOPHIE: There may be a way to escape, but I can't see it.

TOBY: Are you all right – ?

SOPHIE: I can't see anything.
(TOBY fills his glass and goes.
SOPHIE sits at the table, motionless. DIANA comes in in a
rush.
SOPHIE starts.)
Diana –
DIANA: Where did I put it? How silly I am. I had it here. I
put it down in a safe place. Oh, where did I put it? (*She
searches around.*)
SOPHIE: When you tell me to leave Ben – where could I
go? Can you think where I could go?
DIANA: Do help, Sophie, where's my car key? I've left my
car in the drive and people keep on nearly bumping into
it. What's that bread doing on the floor?
SOPHIE: Where, Diana? Where? How do people do it? I'm
such a fool. How do people leave people?
DIANA: I know it was a safe place – I can remember saying
so as I put it down. To myself.
SOPHIE: Diana, can you hear? How do people leave
people?
DIANA: Not aloud. I didn't say it aloud. I was – Of course.
The silver drawer. (*She opens the silver drawer and finds her
key.*) Of course – it's all right, Sophie, you can stop
looking.
(DIANA rushes out.)
SOPHIE: (*Staring at nothing, quietly, dispassionately.*) No-one.
Nowhere. Nothing. No-one. (*Pause. She is suddenly
galvanized, rises, goes to the dresser for the note-pad, writes on
it, then props it on the kitchen table.*)
(SOPHIE goes to the door to the house, opens it and exits.
Long pause.
*VICTORIA and BEN enter from the house; BEN carrying
his tray. They are quarrelling.*)
VICTORIA: What do you mean, perhaps he's had the taste
to leave the house? What do you mean?
BEN: (*Putting the tray by the sink and hurling the remains of his
egg into the waste-bin.*) *Another* uneatable egg!

VICTORIA: Was there a quarrel? What have you done to
　　Charles?

BEN: I'm starving. No-one cares.

VICTORIA: What happened to Charles?

BEN: (*Looking straight at her.*) He was made aware that your
　　husband and I were both cognizant of the blatant and
　　unseemly manner in which the two of you have been
　　comporting yourselves under my roof while enjoying my
　　hospitality.

VICTORIA: (*Sitting down with a thump.*) He's gone –

BEN: No such luck. I should be delighted if you both went,
　　but Charles would never take you on as a permanency.

VICTORIA: Say he hasn't gone –

BEN: Has he asked you to run away with him? (*Silence.*) Of
　　course he hasn't. Why should he, when he can have you
　　here whenever he wants you at no trouble or expense,
　　and leave when he gets bored?
　　(*Silence.*)

VICTORIA: He hasn't gone? Not gone? Say he hasn't gone.

BEN: He'll be having a walk. Working out how to stay here
　　without losing face. Then he'll come in and say to Diana,
　　'What can I do to help you? Let me dance with the left-
　　out ones – let me take that tray up to Michael – you're
　　doing too much.' He'll be helpful, thoughtful, kind.
　　Make Diana grateful. Make her laugh. Then he'll be able
　　to tell himself and you – that although it goes against the
　　grain to stay in the house of anyone as unmannerly as
　　myself, unfortunately his sister-in-law needs him so
　　much that he has no alternative but to put up with it.
　　(*Silence.*) You have nothing to say.

VICTORIA: What can I say?

BEN: Nothing?

VICTORIA: It's true.

BEN: No alleviating circumstances?

VICTORIA: No.

BEN: No comforting lies?

VICTORIA: None. Except that if Toby had got away from this house he might have grown up – been different. We might have been – all right. When I married him I meant to be true, loving and faithful until death.

BEN: We all meant something like that.

VICTORIA: It might have been all right. Unless Charles had come along, of course.

BEN: Why did you pick on that toadying lightweight? He's so boring.

VICTORIA: Is he? I hadn't noticed.

BEN: You've nothing in common –

VICTORIA: (*Suddenly, violently.*) – except entrails. (*Silence.*) Entrails, intertwined, and writhing. (*Pause. She continues conversationally.*) You say he's boring. I daresay. I haven't noticed. I'm not interested in his mind.

(*BEN lifts his eyes to heaven.*)

Why do you sneer? How dare you sneer? How dare you pretend that you don't know about this – this *condition* – when I've seen you white and sick with it? You, you, you yourself. (*Pause.*) I've known you for thirteen years. I know you really quite well. And I've seen you, Ben. I've seen you after Dan Fielding's wife. I've seen you after the woman over at Lacklands – prancing. I've seen you – insane of this, this *love-disease*. You of all people know that it's like scarlet fever or measles – no-one can he blamed for catching it.

BEN: I daresay. But it's ludicrous, it's embarrassing, it's –

VICTORIA: – not nice. Not nice at all. A bitch on heat. (*She turns on him.*) But it's surprised *you* before, hasn't it? Hasn't it? And may do again. (*Pause.*) A gentleman surprised by passion. Deranged. Off the rails. I'm off the rails, Ben. Quite off the rails. I might do anything. (*She exclaims.*) Husband? Children? I've no time for them. They're – in my way. They stand between me and the light. Charles is the light.

(*Silence.*)

BEN: I'm sorry.

VICTORIA: (*Ironically.*) Oh, thank you, thank you.

BEN: Hang on. That's all you can do. Hang on and wait for old age. It'll pass.

VICTORIA: *Pass?*

BEN: Well, it never lasts, does it?

VICTORIA: Of course it will last.

BEN: But.

VICTORIA: What?

BEN: Look around you.

VICTORIA: What at?

BEN: Other people who've – caught it. Last year's passion this year is – spent?

VICTORIA: Oh, yes, but that's other people. (*Pause.*) This is different.

BEN: Different?

VICTORIA: Permanent.
(*Silence.*)

BEN: How can you believe that?

VICTORIA: (*Surprised.*) Because it's true.

BEN: But it doesn't last for anyone else – why should it last for you?

VICTORIA: Because it's different.

BEN: You're about forty. In ten years' time you'll be fifty. I haven't met many fifty-year-olds lately who were burning for anyone. There may be one or two. But sixty-year-olds?

VICTORIA: If I were ninety-five my stomach would rise up and hit my heart when he came near. It's a diseased condition –

BEN: – which you embrace.
(*Pause.*)

VICTORIA: Yes – it shows me things I'd never seen.

BEN: Things? What things?

VICTORIA: Lights – colours – the world. Just the world. Just the whole world. (*Pause.*) I think I should die if it happened all the time. I quite often feel – since Charles came – that I may just die. Just – die. (*Silence.*) What *is* all that bread doing?

BEN: Signposting another failure of a husband and wife to behave towards each other rationally, kindly, or with love. (*Silence. He starts rummaging in a cupboard.*) I need food. Ah. (*He produces a packet and studies it.*) Cheese. (*Pause.*) Christ – listen to this. In French, of course, the language of seduction and general carry-on. 'It charms the palate – applies itself to pleasing you – seduces the most discriminating gourmets.' (*He hurls the packet on the ground.*) I don't ask much. But I do prefer a little reticence from my cheese. Is that unreasonable? Asking too much? Why didn't Sophie buy a quiet, well-behaved chunk of Canadian Cheddar? One of the old school, trained like a Roman, never to show emotion, never to flinch? I will not have cheeses slavering all over me – guttersnipe, pariah, mongrel, *foreign* cheese.

(*VICTORIA reads the note, and rises.*)

VICTORIA: Sophie –

BEN: And I daresay it was very expensive.

VICTORIA: Ben –

BEN: What?

VICTORIA: Sophie –

BEN: What about her?

VICTORIA: She's taken an overdose.

(*Curtain.*)

ACT II

The same. A short while later.

When the CURTAIN rises BEN and DIANA are lugging the unconscious SOPHIE round the kitchen table. VICTORIA is making coffee. TOBY, glass in hand, is sitting on the horse; throughout the following he rocks gently, never taking his eyes off SOPHIE.

DIANA: I know Sophie is often rather thoughtless, but this is the limit.

BEN: We *must* get the doctor.

DIANA: She's just not trying.

BEN: Don't you realize she may die?

DIANA: So like her not to exert herself.

BEN: Supposing she dies?

DIANA: She always has time for that painting of hers – work, she calls it –

BEN: Supposing she dies?

DIANA: – but ask her to do anything that *normal* people call work, and it's quite a different story. (*Briskly.*) Come along now, Sophie. It won't do, you know, dear. You're not helping very much, are you?

BEN: Diana!

DIANA: Yes, Ben, what is it?

BEN: Will you *listen?*

DIANA: I am listening, don't be silly.

BEN: Supposing she –

DIANA: Anyone would think I'm the sort of person who never listens.

BEN: (*Shouting.*) Supposing she dies! *Dies! Dies!*

DIANA: There's no need to shout.

BEN: *Answer,* then!

DIANA: Of course she won't die. She was very clever and brought it all up.
(*BEN looks nauseated.*)

BEN: Then why does she look so – so – dead? Ugh –

DIANA: She's doing splendidly.

BEN: Oh, right as rain.

DIANA: Don't fuss so, Ben. She's got to exert herself a little, to – to – come back.

BEN: If only the doctor –

DIANA: Once and for all, Ben, I am not having doctors and ambulances in the middle of the children's dance. Don't be absurd.

(*VICTORIA examines a picture on the window-sill.*)

BEN: But Sophie –

DIANA: – has been a very silly girl, but now she's going to pull herself together.

BEN: But –

DIANA: *No.*

(*They glare at each other over SOPHIE's inanimate form.*)

BEN: She is my wife.

DIANA: This is no time to think about yourself, Ben. Try and think about Sophie for a change.

BEN: Good God, what do you think I –

DIANA: (*Interrupting.*) She needs a little coffee, that's all. Where is it, Victoria, isn't it ready yet?

(*Pause. VICTORIA still examines the picture.*)

Victoria.

VICTORIA: Mm? Oh yes – here it is. (*She pours out a cup and hands it to DIANA.*)

DIANA: That's far too hot, Victoria, do try and have a little sense. We don't want to give her a nasty burn, do we?

VICTORIA: I'll blow on it. (*She goes back to the picture.*) This is – extraordinary.

DIANA: What is? Oh, that. That's only one of Sophie's little things.

VICTORIA: (*Still studying it.*) It's amazing.

DIANA: Amazing? It's only a tree.

VICTORIA: Only a tree. But I'd never seen it before.

DIANA: Don't be absurd, Victoria, You see that tree every day of your life. It's the elm at the bottom of the kitchen garden.

VICTORIA: I know. But look – look, what Sophie's seen. She's seen it – for the first time, that tree. She's showing it to us – for the first time.

DIANA: I can't say I admire it. It's too empty.

VICTORIA: Empty?

DIANA: If only she'd put one of the dogs in. Brutus would have looked very nice.

VICTORIA: Lifting his leg, I suppose.

DIANA: Don't he vulgar, Victoria. Or perhaps one of the children – yes, Emma in her red sweater. That's it. Painters always like a touch of red in a composition. For a splash of colour. A focus, they call it.

VICTORIA: What absolute nonsense.

DIANA: Excuse me, Victoria, but I do know about these things. After all, I was at school with Dora Chillick. (*Pause.*)

VICTORIA: Who's she?

DIANA: You've never heard of Dora Chillick?

VICTORIA: Never.

DIANA: But she's so well known. She exhibits at the Royal Academy quite regularly. I mean, her paintings *sell*.

VICTORIA: And she always has a splash of colour?

DIANA: Oh, always. That's why her paintings sell so well. And of course, having been at school with her, I know all about it.

VICTORIA: Why?

DIANA: Don't be silly, Victoria, it seeped into me. These things do if you let them. Like lovely music.
(*Silence. VICTORIA looks intently at the painting. Suddenly she turns to SOPHIE – urgent, urgent.*)

VICTORIA: Sophie, come back – come back. How *can* you give up? We need you – to show us. Don't take your eyes away – come back. Come back.

BEN: Thank you, Victoria. I'm glad someone's got the
point.
(*TOBY still rocks gently, his eyes on SOPHIE as she is walked
round the table.*)
TOBY: Is she there? Are you sure she's there?
BEN: What do you mean?
TOBY: Can she hear? Can she think? Can she speak? Or is
there – nothing there?
DIANA: Of course she's there, Toby. Don't be ridiculous.
TOBY: All right, all right, don't snap my head off. All I'm
saying is that she doesn't appear to be with us. Giving in
fact, a remarkable imitation of an absent friend. (*He raises
his glass.*) Absent friends, and God save us all.
DIANA: Oh, stop it, Toby.
TOBY: Yes, but there's her *mind,* you see. Not here – not
there – then where?
DIANA: You can come down off Socrates and have some
coffee, Toby. You and Victoria are going to have to take
your turn at walking Sophie, and I'd rather you didn't
fall over.
TOBY: (*Coming down and pouring coffee.*)
We seek her here.
We seek her there.
We seek her almost everywhere.
Is she in heaven?
Is she in hell –
Or is she just a whippoorwill?
BEN: We can't leave her with Toby in this state.
DIANA: We must, Ben. We can't desert the children
altogether. Anything may happen. Are you all right,
Toby?
TOBY: Right as a trivet. Merry as – as a – (*He frowns and
sways.*)
BEN: We've been going round this table for fifty minutes.
Supposing every one of those minutes was vital.
Supposing –
TOBY: – *lark.*

DIANA: (*Interrupting.*) Look, she brought it all up, it's all *right*. Come on, Toby, we're changing over. Now, Victoria, you take my side.

(*DIANA passes her side of SOPHIE to VICTORIA; BEN passes his over to TOBY.*)

(*To VICTORIA.*) We'll be back in a minute as long as the children are happy. Just keep her walking.

(*DIANA goes out to the house.*

BEN follows her to the door, then turns and puts out a tentative hand to SOPHIE.)

BEN: Oh, *hell* –

(*BEN exits.*

VICTORIA and TOBY stand still for a second, holding SOPHIE. VICTORIA looks anxiously at TOBY as they start walking.)

VICTORIA: You are all right, Toby? You won't suddenly fall over?

TOBY: It would take a far more determined character than I am to stay drunk in circumstances like these.

(*They walk SOPHIE round in silence.*)

VICTORIA: (*Stopping.*) We could try the coffee. (*She sits with SOPHIE below the table.*)

(*Between them, they get the cup to SOPHIE's lips; she makes a choking noise.*)

TOBY: Well, she's in there somewhere.

VICTORIA: Why?

TOBY: She choked.

VICTORIA: You don't think it was a – death rattle?

TOBY: Oh Lord –

VICTORIA: I'm frightened. Are you?

TOBY: Petrified.

VICTORIA: (*Shouting.*) Sophie – Sophie – do come back. Look, Diana says you're perfectly all right, and you know she's never wrong. So you've got to come back, you haven't any choice. (*Pause.*) Diana – says – you're – all right. (*Pause.*) Oh, don't be silly, Sophie, it's only this morning you had your hair washed. You can't die on the

day you had your hair washed, it's absurd. (*Pause. Firmly.*)
Sophie. Sophie. I'm getting rather angry. We want you to
have coffee with us. (*Pause.*) Sophie – Sophie – you're
being very selfish. (*Pause. She begins to cry.*) You're making
me cry, blast you.

TOBY: (*Proffering his handkerchief.*) Nerves.

VICTORIA: What?

TOBY: Making you cry. Nerves.

VICTORIA: I don't care what it is. I don't like it. Oh, come
back, you silly girl, how can you be so *stupid*? Look –
look at that tree. (*She pulls SOPHIE round so that if she
were conscious she would be looking at the tree drawing.*) *You*
drew it – you *saw* it. Look – look at the life streaming
out of it. How dare you try and kill yourself when you
know about that life – look how sacred it is. How
cowardly, how feeble – how *dare* you? Come back!
Come back at once!

(*MICHAEL VERNEY, DIANA's husband, enters from the
house. He is about ten years older than DIANA. At the moment
he is bowed down with 'flu and self pity, and is wearing an
ancient and disreputable dressing-gown.*)

TOBY: Michael, Sophie's –

MICHAEL: Diana promised me coffee an hour and a half
ago. (*He makes for the coffee and pours himself a cup.*)
Coming to something if a man with 'flu can't have a cup
of coffee. (*Pause.*) Sophie had one over the eight? More
your line, Toby.

VICTORIA: She's taken an overdose.

MICHAEL: Overdose, eh? Very impetuous. (*He makes for
the door.*)

VICTORIA: Michael, don't you care at all?

MICHAEL: Care? What about?

VICTORIA: (*Furiously.*) Sophie!

MICHAEL: Sophie? (*Pause.*) Oh, you mean the overdose.
She won't bring it off. Not Sophie. She'll have got the
dose wrong. Anyhow, I daresay Diana's taken her in
hand. Hasn't she?

VICTORIA: Yes, but –

MICHAEL: There you are, then. Anyone Diana takes in
hand is bound to be all right. She'll be as merry as a
cricket in an hour or so. Well, I'm off to bed. Got to be
careful. Don't want a cold on top of this 'flu.
(*MICHAEL exits.*
Silence. VICTORIA talks to SOPHIE calmly.)

VICTORIA: Did you hear that? Michael says you're
perfectly all right. You're just being rather silly and
obstinate. (*She turns on TOBY in a sudden fury.*) If only
you weren't so drunk and ineffectual you'd – you'd – do
something!

TOBY: What?

VICTORIA: *Something!*
(*Pause.*)

TOBY: Cold water on her forehead?

VICTORIA: That's no good.

TOBY: Anything's worth a try.

VICTORIA: Oh, all right.
(*TOBY fetches a mug of water from the sink and splashes
some on SOPHIE's face.*)
(*With intense excitement.*) Toby – Toby – did you see?

TOBY: She nearly spoke.

VICTORIA: Didn't she? Didn't she?

TOBY: I *think* she's –

VICTORIA: More water. (*Silence.*) No. She's gone again. But
she was here – just for a moment.

TOBY: Did you see her eyes?

VICTORIA: Yes. There was life in them. Oh, what a relief,
Toby, and it was all your idea. How clever of you.
(*Silence.*)

TOBY: I can't remember how long it is since you've spoken
to me like that. As though I were – a human being. You
spoke – to me. (*Silence.*) Yes. Well. One of those flukes.
(*He lifts SOPHIE. They start walking her round again.*)
(*After a pause.*) Victoria, if I – got a job – did something
– would you be – pleased?

VICTORIA: You're always talking about getting a job.

TOBY: But if I did – would you be with me? (*Silence.*) You can't answer that. Don't try.

(*DIANA and BEN enter.*)

DIANA: Sophie! You're not still being silly?

VICTORIA: It's all right – she nearly came to. There was a distinct flicker.

DIANA: Flicker?

VICTORIA: Of life.

BEN: You're sure?

VICTORIA: Oh yes.

BEN: Quite sure?

VICTORIA: Yes.

BEN: So she's perfectly all right.

DIANA: What are you talking about, Ben? I keep on telling you Sophie's all right. She's just being rather obstinate and unhelpful, but then of course, she always was.

BEN: (*Furiously, glaring at SOPHIE.*) There's no need to speak of her in the past. She'll live to exercise her maladress for many years to come.

DIANA: Ben! Only a few minutes ago you were in such a state about her.

BEN: – when I thought she was in danger of dying unshriven of this appalling sin.

VICTORIA: Sin? You can't call Sophie trying to kill herself sin.

BEN: Of course it's sin. In my canon, Dante's and God's –

TOBY: – in ascending order of merit.

DIANA: Really, Ben.

BEN: What do you mean, 'Really, Ben'? Can't I mention God?

DIANA: It's not Sunday, dear.

(*TOBY sits SOPHIE and sits by her. DIANA fetches a cloth and places it under SOPHIE's head.*)

BEN: Do you realize that under Queen Victoria attempted suicide carried the death penalty? Try and slit your throat and fail, and you were patched up quick as lightning so they could hang you.

VICTORIA: You're being nauseating, Ben. (*To herself.*) I wish Charles was here.

DIANA: Sin, indeed. Poor Sophie.

VICTORIA: I think I'll just see if he's back.

(*VICTORIA exits to the house.*)

DIANA: You're talking absolute nonsense, Ben.

BEN: Oh, can't you see? *Why* can't you see? Suicide is despair. Which is sin, It is violence. Violence against the soul. And this too is – sin.

TOBY: You're using rather odd words, Ben. They don't mean much, you know. Not to most people.

BEN: What does that matter, if they are true?

TOBY: I can't myself blame anyone for fancying a little oblivion.

BEN: Oblivion? *Oblivion?* Who can guarantee oblivion? (*Silence.*) Supposing she were to wake up to everlasting life?

DIANA: I wish you wouldn't talk like that, dear. It's not very nice.

BEN: And supposing that when she woke to everlasting life she found herself carrying with her everything she was running from? The intolerable burden of her sins?

TOBY: Myself, I believe in a dead end –

BEN: I wouldn't like to bet on it.

TOBY: – where at least she would have escaped from you.

BEN: I wouldn't bet on that, either.

(*Pause.*)

TOBY: Supposing you go on doing it.

DIANA: Doing it?

TOBY: Throw yourself off a roof – and you keep on doing it – every second – through eternity. Slit your throat – again and again and again. The same hesitation as you feel the razor's edge.

DIANA: Really, Toby, where do you get your nasty morbid ideas?

BEN: He got that one from Dante. Who said it better. (*He
shouts in SOPHIE's ear.*) Are you listening? You're very
lucky that this cowardly attempt of yours has failed.
Because if you had succeeded and this theory were true
you would be in for a very unpleasant time and I would
not be in your shoes for all the money you might care to
offer me. (*In a matter-of-fact tone.*) Or for all the tea in
China, as they say. (*He paces.*)

DIANA: You were too much for her, Ben. You must try and
be a little kinder. She couldn't stand it any more and
suddenly something snapped –

BEN: (*Stopping in exasperation.*) 'Suddenly something
snapped.' I like that. Alliterative. Terse. Apposite. Above
all, original. You must say it more often. A jewelled
phrase like that deserves frequent airing.

DIANA: Don't you feel any pity for her?

BEN: No, I do not. Fury is what I feel. A deep and
passionate anger. Did she give a moment's thought to
anyone but herself? To her children? Her husband? Her
friends? No – no – no is the answer!

DIANA: There's no need to shout.

BEN: There's too much of it about. You see it all the time –
a little unhappiness, a modicum of domestic discontent,
not getting entirely your own way, and it's on with the
gas – head in the oven – down with the pills, a quick bit
of wrist-slitting and hey presto, another opter-out has
slipped his – or her – collar, his mortal coil, and sneaked
out of the back door, leaving those behind bereaved,
bewildered, and overwhelmed with useless, life-
destroying guilt. I hate suicide. Also I think it's
ineffectual. Useless. Because I believe in eternal life, and
if eternal life exists then we must – answer. All of us.
One by one.
(*Silence.*)

DIANA: Really, Ben, you can't have it both ways. If sin and
eternal life and – so forth and so forth – are true, then so
are love and compassion, and you haven't shown Sophie

the faintest glimmerings of either. And although she's
been very thoughtless in her choice of an evening – I
hope you're listening, Sophie – it's entirely due to you
that we have this lifeless object on our hands while the
children dance.

BEN: (*Shouting.*) I will not shoulder *everything* in this house!
I will not pay all the bills *and* be blamed when the
toaster breaks *and* when Sophie tries to kill herself! And
what does she mean by doing it without telling me?
She's got a tongue in her head. She might have
mentioned it in passing.

DIANA: She did mention it. Now and then over the past
seventeen years. Most days, really.

BEN: She moaned a bit –

DIANA: We've all told you for years. But you just went on
talking.

BEN: If my wife is going to commit suicide I expect her to
mention it in passing. Over the toast and marmalade.
While cleaning her teeth. Heavens, surely she can find a
moment? (*Pause.*) Why today, for heaven's sake? Nothing
happened –

TOBY: What about the telephone call?

BEN: What telephone call?

TOBY: The telephone call she overheard.

BEN: Who told you about that? Did she?

DIANA: No-one had to tell us. You were shouting about it.
Everyone in the house knows.

TOBY: You may not realize it, but you lack reticence.

BEN: But that was totally unimportant.

TOBY: To whom?

BEN: To me, of course.

DIANA: But not to her.

BEN: It's no use making frivolous excuses for her. She's
done this because she neither feared God nor loved man.
And when she comes to I am going to teach her at least
to fear God.

TOBY: (*Going to the whisky.*) Between fear of God and terror of you she won't know where to turn. (*He pours a drink.*)

BEN: There will be no repetition of this nonsense. She can stick it out to the end like the rest of us. (*Pause. To SOPHIE.*) Do you hear? You can stick it out to the end like the rest of us!

DIANA: (*To TOBY.*) Oh Toby, not *another* –

TOBY: (*Mounting the horse.*) Another. And another. And another. But I'm like Sophie. No short cut to oblivion.

BEN: Oblivion is not to be had so easily.

TOBY: That had not escaped me. But I keep on trying. Battle of Britain spirit.

(*VICTORIA enters.*)

VICTORIA: He's *nowhere.*

DIANA: Who?

BEN: (*Exasperated.*) My dear Diana –

VICTORIA: I've looked all over the house.

DIANA: What's she talking about?

BEN: How naive you are.

TOBY: Charles. She's talking about Charles.

VICTORIA: It's not like him –

BEN: He'll be back. Comfortable house. Easy living.
(*BEN lifts SOPHIE, DIANA goes to her other side.*)
God, she's getting heavy. This'll ruin my back. When she comes to she can go on a diet.

DIANA: Don't be silly. She's as light as a feather.

BEN: (*Shouting at SOPHIE.*) Do you hear? You can go on a diet and get some of that weight off.
(*DIANA and BEN start walking SOPHIE round again.*)
And I'm hungry. (*Pause.*) I suppose your husband has dined. He knows how to look after himself –

DIANA: You're not to be horrid about Michael.

BEN: I have the deepest respect for your husband, and unqualified admiration for the way he avoids anything unpleasant by going to bed and staying there until the all clear.

DIANA: He's very delicate.

BEN: School sports, boring neighbours, the children's dance – he can always run up a temporary illness which never stops him eating or drinking and provides you with healthy exercise running up and downstairs with trays. I hold no brief for the generally held theory that he's a fool.

DIANA: He's not.

BEN: I agree. He's a very clever man. And he got his supper tonight, unlike the rest of us.

DIANA: You're being –

BEN: Didn't he?

DIANA: Certainly I took him up a little liver. He needs it.

BEN: *And* a little strengthening claret?

DIANA: Do you grudge him a glass of wine?

BEN: A *glass?*

DIANA: There's no sense in keeping an open bottle until the next day.

BEN: My best Château Léoville-Poyferré I suppose. No, I'm not complaining. I'm only asking what there is for us? (*Pause.*)

DIANA: Sausage rolls.
(*Silence.*)

BEN: (*Very quietly.*) Sausage rolls. How are we to support an abortive suicide on sausage rolls?

TOBY: Had Diana known that Sophie was going to try and do away with herself the knowledge would no doubt have been reflected in the menu.

BEN: She could have guessed that *something* would go wrong. It always does, after all. It happened to be Sophie, but it might have been you drunk and insulting the guests, or fire breaking out – but it is always something. This is not a house where you can afford to serve sausage rolls *at any time.* Because here stomachs are endlessly churning. Here the gastric juices are never allowed to run a quiet, leisurely course. They are for ever on the jolt. I daresay there are well-ordered establishments where you could serve cheesecake, sausage rolls and plum pudding at every meal without arousing more than a faint hiccup. But in this house stomachs need cosseting if they are to keep up with the strain of violent and emotional living.

DIANA: And whose fault is that?

BEN: Oh, mine, mine, of course, mine – like everything else that goes wrong –

(*CHARLES enters from outside.*)

VICTORIA: Where were you? Where have you been?

CHARLES: Good heavens – what's the matter with Sophie?

VICTORIA: I looked everywhere – I thought you'd gone.

DIANA: Overdose.

CHARLES: Intentional?

DIANA: Yes.

CHARLES: Oh my God.

VICTORIA: I thought you'd gone.

CHARLES: Diana, poor Diana, how awful for you. What can I do to help?

BEN: (*To VICTORIA.*) Dance with the left-out ones – take that tray up to Michael. (*Pause.*) Satisfied?

CHARLES: (*Ignoring him.*) When's the doctor coming?

DIANA: He's not.

CHARLES: *What?*

DIANA: Ben won't have him.

CHARLES: *Won't?*

BEN: (*Snarling.*) Won't. Won't. Won't.

DIANA: (*Hastily.*) Charles, would you like to look at the children? I don't like leaving them.

BEN: Why should he look at the children? I'll go.

DIANA: We'll both go. Victoria, will you take over from me, dear? (*She hands her half of SOPHIE to VICTORIA.*)

VICTORIA: (*Taking it.*) Charles will help me.

CHARLES: Of course. (*He takes BEN's side.*)

(*BEN glares at CHARLES, but CHARLES ignores him.*)

DIANA: We won't be long – just have a quick look. (*She looks at SOPHIE.*) You must do better than this, Sophie.

(*DIANA and BEN go out to the house.*

VICTORIA looks at TOBY. Silence.)

VICTORIA: (*Exasperated.*) Toby.

TOBY: Mm? (*Pause.*) Oh. You mean I'm here. Ah. (*Pause. He dismounts.*) Better find somewhere else, hadn't I?

CHARLES: Don't go.

(*TOBY gets to the door, then returns for the whisky bottle.*)

TOBY: My dear chap. Don't let your finer feelings embarrass you.

(*TOBY exits.*)

CHARLES: (*Angrily.*) I wish you wouldn't talk to Toby like that.

VICTORIA: Where were you?

CHARLES: It makes everything so difficult for me – I won't be able to come here any more if you can't behave better.

VICTORIA: Charles!

CHARLES: Do have a little sense.

VICTORIA: Charles, take me with you.

(*Pause.*)

CHARLES: Where on earth to?

VICTORIA: Anywhere if you're there.

CHARLES: My dear girl, you're behaving very strangely. You can hardly see me as a home-maker? A nest-builder? I've never understood what makes people put two twigs together. You be a sensible girl. Stay with Toby and keep a roof over your head.

VICTORIA: Charles –

CHARLES: And stop ordering him about like that. It's ugly.

(*Silence.*)

VICTORIA: Ben was right. I simply pass the time for you.

CHARLES: What a vulgar way to talk.

VICTORIA: It's true. Just a – a sex object.

CHARLES: Is that a term of abuse? I don't think so. But if you don't like it, the years will mend it. Soon enough.

(*Silence. They stand still and look at each other.*)

VICTORIA: Oh, get out of my marrow. Get out, get *out!*

CHARLES: Want me to go?

VICTORIA: No. (*Pause.*) Want me?

CHARLES: Yes.

VICTORIA: Now?

CHARLES: Yes. But we have other business.

VICTORIA: Damn.

CHARLES: Later.

VICTORIA: Can't we just drop her? She's quite all right now really, you know.

CHARLES: Of course we can't. (*Pause.*) Later.

(*Pause.*)

VICTORIA: Damn Sophie.

(*They start walking again.*)

CHARLES: Ben was bloody rude this evening. If I didn't think Diana sometimes needed a bit of help I wouldn't stay here.

(*Silence.*)

VICTORIA: Damn Ben. Damn and blast him. And damn you.

(*BEN and DIANA come in, followed by TOBY.*
There is a loud noise of music until BEN shuts the door.
DIANA looks at SOPHIE and stops.)

DIANA: Sophie, you're not *still* being silly? (*Pause.*) This is no time to be funny. (*Pause.*) We're all getting rather cross with you. You're giving us a lot of trouble. I – (*She suddenly goes nearer SOPHIE and looks attentively at her.*)

CHARLES: What's the matter?

BEN: What's the *matter?*

(*Panic. They all crowd round SOPHIE.*)

DIANA: Look – she's not supporting herself any longer. They're carrying her.

BEN: Get her on the table.

(*They put SOPHIE on the table.*)

CHARLES: *Why* didn't you get a doctor? This is going to look terrible.

VICTORIA: She's dead.

TOBY: Of course she isn't dead.

VICTORIA: Oh my God –

CHARLES: Mind her head.

DIANA: Give me a glass. Victoria, give me a glass.
   (*VICTORIA gives DIANA the glass out of her handbag. DIANA
   holds it to SOPHIE's nostrils. A long silence.*)

VICTORIA: Well?

   (*Silence.*)

TOBY: Is she – (*Simultaneously with VICTORIA.*) dead?

VICTORIA: (*Simultaneously with TOBY.*) – breathing?
   (*BEN gives SOPHIE the kiss of life. Silence. He repeats it
   four times.*)

DIANA: There's nothing – nothing there.

CHARLES: (*On BEN's third kiss of life.*) Oh my God, it's
   impossible. What can we do?

DIANA: (*Putting the glass down.*) Oh Sophie, Sophie, be
   sensible.

VICTORIA: Slap her – shake her – throw water over her.
   (*BEN hits SOPHIE's heart – gives pulse compression. They
   all gasp.*)

DIANA: Ben – what are you doing?

TOBY: He's going to bring her back.

VICTORIA: (*To TOBY.*) Surely it's – dangerous.

TOBY: Leave him alone.

DIANA: Sophie, the children – think of the children.

VICTORIA: Sophie –

TOBY: Come on, Soph, fight, fight – come on back.
   (*BEN gives her the kiss of life again, twice. The others stand
   frozen. He starts massaging again.*)

CHARLES: She's turning blue.

VICTORIA: Her fingers are blue.

TOBY: Come *on!* Come *on!* You're still there. Come – on!
   Come – home! Fight. Fight.

DIANA: Oh God, bring her back.

TOBY: Come – *on!*

BEN: The glass.

VICTORIA: (*Holding the glass to SOPHIE.*) There's nothing
   there.

DIANA: Help. God – help Sophie – Sophie – help – help –
God.

VICTORIA: Sophie – the children – think – the children.
(*She shouts in SOPHIE's ear.*) Come out of that limbo –
come back – come – back – (*Her voice fades away.*)

DIANA: Thy will be done. Thy will be done –

VICTORIA: Only if it's to bring her back. Bring back her
mind, God, and make her body twitch.

CHARLES: Breathe – breathe –
(*Total silence. BEN goes on massaging. They are all frozen as
though about to run a race. The silence is long.*)

TOBY: (*Urgently.*) We *want* you back. We want *you* back.
(*Silence.*) Ben, do something. Do more. You can always
do anything. Get her back, Ben. Force her back. You can
do it. (*Pause. To VICTORIA, confidently.*) You'll see – he
can do anything when he really tries.
(*BEN goes on massaging. A long silence. Eventually he stands
back, panting. VICTORIA crouches by SOPHIE. Silence.*)

BEN: The glass. The glass.
(*VICTORIA holds the glass to SOPHIE's nostrils. A long
silence.*)

VICTORIA: It's – clouding. Look. Look, Diana. Look,
Charles, look – look at the beautiful clouds. It's life.
Only minutes ago there was – nothing. Now – look at
that life. (*She embraces DIANA.*) Life – life – lovely life.
(*She holds up the glass again and pulls DIANA to look at it.*)
You see, don't you – how strong it is. Wake up, Sophie,
wake up, it's a new world. Do you hear, Sophie? A new
world.

BEN: She can rest for a few minutes. She'll do.
(*They all stagger as though drunk. BEN, yawning, puts his
head down on the table and seems to go to sleep.*)

DIANA: Well done, Ben. You did it. Well done.

TOBY: I knew he could do it. If he wanted to. He can do
anything if he wants to.
(*During the next speech VICTORIA wanders round the room,
unable to stay still. She comes suddenly within CHARLES'*)

physical orbit and stands rigid. TOBY watches as they look at
each other, absorbed in each other, sleepwalking.)

DIANA: *Ooooh!* (*She gives a long, drawn-out sigh, and stretches.)*
It was all right, you know. Everything was – marvellous.
They all looked so happy. I wish it could go on for ever
for them. If only time would stop, and everything else –
the music, and the lights, and the dancing – just – flowed
on.

(*CHARLES and VICTORIA exit to the house.*
There is a long silence, then TOBY, moving very suddenly,
bounds at the clock and wrenches off the minute hand.)

TOBY: Then why don't we stop it? What's time ever done
for us? Are we to feel grateful for the havoc it's brought
us? If it weren't for time, everything would be – like it
was. There. How silly it looks. It's – it's – (*Waving*
towards the clock.) – dead.

DIANA: (*In exasperation, not surprise.)* Oh, *Toby* –
(*TOBY wrenches off the hour hand.)*

TOBY: No more minutes. No more hours. It's totally done
for. Quite – pathetic. Time – was.

DIANA: That's the third time since Christmas you've
broken the clock.

TOBY: You don't understand. It hasn't done anything for us.
Ever. What's it given us? Marriage. *Marriage.*

DIANA: It's so hard explaining to Tibbits why the hands
keep breaking.

TOBY: Treachery, blackness, damnation – presents from
time, tastefully gift-wrapped. (*Shouting at the clock.)* Take
them back! Whatever you have to offer, I don't want.
You've *nothing* for me.

DIANA: You've got the horrors again, Toby, and I really
can't stand it.

TOBY: (*Shouting into the shadows.)* Mrs Eppings! Mrs
Eppings! You can come out now. Time's stopped.
(*Menacingly.)* I know you're there, Mrs Eppings. Why
don't you answer? I want to know about those lies.
(*Pause.)* James! James! Did you hate us, James? (*Pause.)*

Don't you hear, you can all come out now. (*Pointing to the clock.*) It's – dead.

DIANA: There's no-one there, Toby.

TOBY: Don't be silly, they're all there. The room's crowded.

DIANA: They're *buried,* dear. Over there – (she *points vaguely.*) – in the churchyard. They're very – contented. They have lovely flowers growing out of them. Snowdrops and so forth. Very nice.

TOBY: Their mouths are stopped with snowdrops.

DIANA: And the children do the weeding. They're very good about it.

TOBY: Crowded – they're all around us. There's no room for a soul to breathe – jostle, jostle, every inch taken. (*Pause.*) Gross overcrowding. (*In a matter-of-fact tone.*) Slum conditions, really.

DIANA: (*Shaking BEN.*) Ben, Toby's got the horrors again.

TOBY: (*Lunging into a dark corner.*) I see you!

DIANA: It's the second time this evening, and it's too much. (*Pause.*) Can't we have him dried out or something?

TOBY: James –

BEN: (*Lifting his head from his hands and looking at TOBY.*) Is there anything left to dry out?

DIANA: Of course there is. He doesn't have the horrors all the time. They'll be gone in five minutes.
(*Silence, while BEN examines TOBY, who is looking into dark corners and muttering.*)

TOBY: Mrs Eppings, Martha, Jenny –
(*TOBY exits through the pantry opening.*)

BEN: He could be dried out, I suppose. But nothing will bring him back to life if he doesn't want to come. He's doing a Sophie.

DIANA: Doing a – ?

BEN: Suicide is what he's up to. He's killing his mind and body because he can't stand the pain.

DIANA: *What* pain?

BEN: Being alive. He always flinched at everything, don't
you remember? Finding a dead blackbird, lack of love,
unkindness – growing up. Now he's flinching on a rather
larger scale. (*Dispassionately.*) I think he's beyond help.

DIANA: Don't say that, Ben. He's so nice. So loving. He
can't be so far gone –

BEN: (*Exploding.*) When I think what I meant life in this
house to be – and what it is. I meant us all to be so *happy*.
A family commune, an answer to the horrors of modern
life in a mad world. The family – like a clenched fist –
guns pointing outwards.

DIANA: You were quite right, Ben. Look at the children.

BEN: Yes. But what about us? Toby – Sophie – you –

DIANA: Me? I'm perfectly all right.

BEN: You've never been all right since Simon jilted you.
Twenty years ago.
(*Silence.*)

DIANA: My hands have got very rough. I must put some
cream on them.

BEN: So it's still a green wound. (*Pause.*) If only you'd take
it out and look at it closely it would become stale –
familiar. It would stop eating you. (*Pause.*) Forty isn't too
old to start growing again. But you must – know –
your – demons.
(*Silence.*)

DIANA: I saw him. About a year ago.

BEN: Where?

DIANA: In London. He was walking down Bond Street in
front of me. I hadn't seen him since – since –

BEN: What?

DIANA: He was fat. He'd lost a lot of hair. He looked
prosperous. But I felt – (*She pauses.*)

BEN: What did you feel?
(*Pause.*)

DIANA: Young. Desperate. (*Silence.*) Just – the same. Like I
haven't felt for twenty years. Alive. Trembling. Terrified.

BEN: Did you speak to him?

DIANA: *No.* (*Silence.*) I went into the Ritz and was sick down the lavatory. (*Silence.*) I hadn't changed, you see. (*Silence.*) Don't undermine me, Ben. Because I love Michael, I love my children, and I'm more than reconciled to life. I enjoy most days. So just leave it to lie.
(*BEN stretches out a hand and puts it over hers. Silence.*)
And what about you?

BEN: (*After a pause.*) I would be all right – I suppose – if when I came home at the week-end I had love. With love you can do anything. But when I arrive on Friday evening, no-one actually has any time for me. And I'm not generous enough – to be happy watching a family going about its own concerns with no thoughts for me. I go back on Monday more tired than when I came down. And I am unfaithful to my wife, not because of the lusts of the flesh, but because I need love – no, don't say it. You're right, I haven't found it. Well, *why* can't I get love? What's the matter with me? No, don't tell me that either. If you need love you don't get it. Let your need be total and you'll drive everyone away – they'll *run*. And my need appals my wife, so she – runs. Tonight we've had the longest run yet. Escape from Colditz. But the Gauleiter brought her back. (*Glaring at SOPHIE.*) Snarl, snarl, gloat, gloat. (*Pause.*) I saw the greengrocer and his wife out for a walk. They've been married for forty years. He has no hair – no teeth – but they were holding hands. No-one holds my hand. I can neither win love nor grow reconciled to being without it. Can't get used to the idea. (*Urgently.*) Tell me how to win love or live without it.

DIANA: You're surrounded by it.

BEN: The dogs get more affection than I do. They're fondled, cherished – who fondles me? (*Bitterly.*) And why should anyone?

DIANA: You're just being sorry for yourself. Now, if you were weak like me –

BEN: *Weak? You?* My dear Diana. A combination of Joan of Arc, Hercules and Popeye. After Simon left you, you built yourself. What a construction. An impregnable fortress to shelter the rest of us. An ark –
(*MICHAEL enters.*)

MICHAEL: (*To DIANA, reproachfully.*) Had to get my own coffee. *And* bring the cup down. I thought you might come up with a little brandy.

DIANA: We've been looking after Sophie.

MICHAEL: Never mind, never mind. Here now. Get it myself. (*He rummages for the brandy.*) Sophie all hotsy-totsy again, eh? (*To DIANA.*) If you *really* want to help you can get me a hot water bottle. Sweat this temperature out.

DIANA: (*Resignedly.*) Yes, Michael. I'll get it now.
(*DIANA goes out to the house.*
MICHAEL goes and pours himself a large glass of brandy.
TOBY appears from the pantry, still looking in dark corners.)

MICHAEL: Doesn't look like one of Toby's better evenings.
(*MICHAEL exits to the house.*
As the door is opened, strains of 'Good night, sweetheart' are heard.)

BEN: What on earth are they playing that for? It's one of *our* parents' songs. Part of their nostalgia, I suppose, for what they imagine to have been our carefree youth. Before time was. In the olden days.
(*TOBY closes the door and comes forward, glazed and mechanical, and starts singing.*)

TOBY: 'Good night, sweetheart,
Till we meet tomorrow.
Good night, sweetheart,
Sleep will banish sorrow –'

BEN: But it never does, does it? Wonder if they've noticed.

TOBY: '– Tears and partings.
May make us forlorn.
But with the dawn.

A new day is born –'
(*He comes to with a shiver.*) Christ. A new day.

BEN: Are you with us again?

TOBY: Only on a temporary basis. Purely temporary, my
dear Ben, I assure you.

BEN: While you're here you can help me get Sophie into
the chair. It's time she sat up.

(*BEN and TOBY help SOPHIE into a chair.*)

TOBY: Ben –

BEN: The one lasting result of this evening's gallimaufry
will be permanent injury to my spine.

TOBY: Ben –

BEN: What is it?

TOBY: Tell her you're glad she's back.

BEN: What?

TOBY: Ben –

BEN: Christ! (*He goes and pours a drink.*)

TOBY: (*After a silence.*) What happened, Ben? When did you
change? What happened to the child who used to ride
Socrates? What happened to all that hope? (*Silence.*) You
can have Socrates. If you want him so much. I don't want
him. I want the boy who used to ride him back. I watch
the way you treat Sophie. The child who rode for
Erzerum couldn't have treated anyone like you treat her.
What happened to him? (*Pause.*) Is he dead?

BEN: He put away childish things.

TOBY: Do you remember how we used to dream about
being grown up? Panting with eagerness, yearning – for
this. You so treacherous and unkind that your wife hasn't
the heart to go on living. Diana, a heavy-handed matron,
never dancing or singing any more, Me – ugh – me –

BEN: But the children, Toby – all our children – they're
marvellous.

TOBY: And are they to end like us? Drunken, frivolous, and
middle-aged?

BEN: No, they're better than we were.

TOBY: They're *not* better than we were. Don't you
    remember? What were we like?

BEN: We were like other children.

TOBY: No.
    (*Silence.*)

BEN: What are you on about?
    (*Silence.*)

TOBY: I wanted you to lead me somewhere. (*Pause.*) I
    always knew you would. (*Pause.*) I've always been waiting
    for you to say where we were going. What great
    enterprise. What new Erzerum. I've been waiting in the
    wings. Hanging about. (*Pause.*) Aren't you going to lead
    me anywhere? Ever? Nowhere in the world?

BEN: Toby, I grew up.

TOBY: Grew up.

BEN: *Someone had to.*
    (*Silence.*)

TOBY: No Roland. No Oliver. No Erzerum.

BEN: That's right.

TOBY: You should have told me. It's rather late, isn't it, to
    realize that one's life is built on straw?

BEN: It's *not* too late.

TOBY: Oh, you're strong, Ben. Robust. Nothing's too late
    for you.
    (*SOPHIE mutters something.*)
    What, Sophie? What did you say?

BEN: Probably thanking us brokenly. (*He shouts at
    SOPHIE.*) Speak up!

TOBY: Ben!

BEN: (*To SOPHIE, exploding.*) It's intolerable. We spend a
    miserable evening bringing you back to your senses, we
    ruin our backs, our digestions are shot to pieces, and
    then all you can do is groan. What about a word of
    thanks? A cheery smile? (*Giving up.*) Oh, stick pins in
    her. (*He goes to the dresser for a drink.*)

TOBY: Ben! Don't. Please don't.
    (*Silence.*)

BEN: (*Shouting, overwhelmed.*) Oh, all right, all *right*. Come back, Sophie, come back – newly born – and love me. *Love me.* I need you to hold my hand when my teeth fall out. I need you to cheer me when I'm unhappy, to understand my needs and support my weakness. I need you to comfort me when the world ignores me, when more able men win the prizes that escape me, when younger men race by me. (*He kneels by SOPHIE.*) You've never felt much passion for me, and now, I suppose, you never will. But we have not got *nothing*. Look around at other marriages and then ask who are we to cry stinking fish. Come back, Sophie. I need you for my wife.

(*Very slowly, SOPHIE holds out her hand to BEN. He takes it and kisses it.*)

SOPHIE: I'll – try. (*Pause.*) Heaven help us.

BEN: Yes. Perhaps. I hope.

(*Silence.*)

SOPHIE: It was – cold.

BEN: What was?

SOPHIE: What?

BEN: What was cold?

SOPHIE: I don't know. (*Pause.*) I heard – everything you were saying. All the time. But I couldn't – speak. It was – it was –

BEN: It was what?

SOPHIE: Cold. (*Pause.*) Would I have gone on hearing you after – after – ?

BEN: After you were dead.

SOPHIE: Yes.

BEN: Abstract speculation of that nature pays few dividends.

SOPHIE: Dividends. (*Pause.*) I was wrong, Ben.

BEN: Of course you were wrong.

SOPHIE: I don't know what the answer is.

BEN: We're going to try. That's what the answer is.

SOPHIE: Not easy.

BEN: Of course it's not easy. We're going to have a terrible time.

TOBY: That's right. Cheer her up.

BEN: (*Not listening to TOBY.*) But consider the alternative. And then get down on your knees and pray for strength.
(*DIANA enters.*
Outside there is the noise of voices and laughter.)

DIANA: Come on, Ben, they want to thank you.

BEN: Thank me? (*He rises.*)

DIANA: For having them. Oh, *there* you are. Sophie, back at last – really, you gave us quite a fright, you know, you really shouldn't have done it. But we won't say anything more about it.

SOPHIE: I –

DIANA: We'll just forget it. We all make mistakes. I did exactly the same thing myself once.

BEN / TOBY: (*Speaking together.*) *You* –

DIANA: Yes.
(*Silence.*)

TOBY: Diana – why?

DIANA: Because I thought there was nothing to live for, of course. That's the usual reason, isn't it? Because death seemed such a good idea. Because I couldn't see in front of me the chance of a single day's happiness. (*Briskly.*) I was quite wrong, of course. And so were you. Life is perfectly possible. Come on, Ben, I don't want them all trailing in here to say good-bye.
(*BEN and DIANA go out.*)

TOBY: *Well.*
(*Silence. SOPHIE rises and goes to the sink for a drink of water.*)

SOPHIE: I thought – I thought I knew her.

TOBY: Sophie –

SOPHIE: Mm?

TOBY: I never knew about Diana. (*To himself.*) How *could* she? I never knew – so I couldn't help. I'd like to help you. It won't be easy – you and Ben.

(*SOPHIE sits and picks up her pencil and sketch-book.*)

SOPHIE: Don't move – (*Starts drawing him.*) My mouth
tastes awful.

TOBY: You'll need an ally. We might sometimes – have a
drink together. I'd like someone to have a drink with. We
could – talk.

(*Pause. SOPHIE draws.*)

SOPHIE: What about?

TOBY: Oh-candle-snuffers. Elephant guns.

SOPHIE: *Candle*-snuffers?

TOBY: Anything you like. *Petit point.*

SOPHIE: Why candle-snuffers?

TOBY: It's not much of an offer. But it's meant as a –
bridge.

SOPHIE: A bridge.

TOBY: A small, delicate, but resilient bridge.

(*Pause.*)

SOPHIE: I don't know anything about elephant guns.

TOBY: You would have an ally.

SOPHIE: Or bridges.

TOBY: I'll play you my old seventy-eights if you like.

(*Pause.*)

SOPHIE: I'm not at all musical. (*She throws down her pencil.*)
(*Silence.*)

TOBY: Forget it.

(*Silence. SOPHIE looks at TOBY. She goes and sits by him.
BEN and DIANA enter. The door is open, but there is total
silence outside. They sit down at the table.*)

DIANA: Silence. Lovely silence. They've all gone. (*Pause.*)
Lord, how tired I am. What an evening. *What* an
evening. (*Pause.*) Where are Charles and Victoria? Why
aren't they here?

(*Pause.*)

BEN: Nothing happened.

DIANA: I haven't seen them for ages. Where are they?

BEN: Nothing happened. A few middle-aged people turned
on each other. Blamed each other for not being twenty

any more. Threatened to leave each other. Realized they
would not do better anywhere else. Decided to stay.

DIANA: I suppose they've gone to bed. Odd, not saying
good night.

BEN: Some children had a dance and thought the evening –
the world – would go on for ever. Nothing happened.

SOPHIE: (*Giving an enormous yawn.*) Thank you, Toby. I'd
like that. (*She yawns.*) Elephant guns. (*She puts her head on
TOBY's shoulder and goes fast asleep.*)
(*TOBY looks at her in amazement, then very gently makes
her head more comfortable.*)

BEN: (*Looking at SOPHIE and TOBY.*) A few wounds were
examined. Some were healing nicely. Others were seen
to go deeper. One or two were noticed to be mortal.
Nothing happened. (*He goes to the sink.*)

DIANA: Anyhow. The children had a lovely dance.

BEN: (*Looking out of the window.*) Dawn's breaking. Silence,
and the dawn breaking. (*He laughs.*) Look – come here.
(*DIANA joins him and looks out of the window.*)

DIANA: Oh!

TOBY: What?

DIANA: The children –

TOBY: Haven't they gone home? Perhaps they want
breakfast.

DIANA: No – ours. Oh really, haven't they any sense?

TOBY: Devilled kidneys – kedgeree.

DIANA: They're dancing on the grass. They've got no
shoes on, and they're practically naked. I must go and –

BEN: Leave them.

DIANA: But they'll get pneumonia –

BEN: *Leave them.* (*Restraining her.*) It's their morning.
(*Curtain.*)

ODDS ON OBLIVION

CAST

DOROTHEA DELANEY (AUNT DOLLY),
a professor of genetics

CLIVE WARREN, her nephew

KATE HAMMOND, a social worker

SERGEANT GWYNNE, a detective

TONY GOLDSMITH (LUMPKIN), a bookie

TIME: The present
PLACE: A flat in Soho

Scene One: Early March
Scene Two: Three months later
Scene Three: Twenty minutes later
Scene Four: Five weeks later
Scene Five: Two weeks later

Scene One

The main room of a flat in Soho. About a third of it is a good working kitchen, the rest is for living: an agreeable place to be. Decent early nineteenth century furniture, a round dining/working table, mahogany chairs. Two disreputable armchairs, badly in need of upholstering, but unlikely to get it. Large bookcase, crammed with books, books and papers spilling everywhere; piled on the floor. On the walls, several black and white engravings of horses by Stubbs. A good room; no decorator has ever been near it.

PROFESSOR DELANEY (AUNT DOLLY) and her nephew CLIVE are just coming in, laden with shopping which they are unloading partly by the sink, partly on the table, shoving books aside to make room.

AUNT DOLLY is old, short-sighted. She has enormous energy, and moves very fast. CLIVE, in his early fifties, is low on energy, a nice man with no ambition, agreeable to have around. He puts down the last parcel and takes a deep breath.

CLIVE: High spot of the week, our Saturday shopping.
(*AUNT DOLLY begins peering at parcels, unwrapping things, putting them away.*)
You must know everyone in Soho, they all talk to you.
(*He begins to unwrap things, very slowly. He is as slow as she is fast.*)
They never talk to me. Well, I wouldn't know what to say if they did.
(*Unwraps a parcel of carrots.*)
Nice carrots.
(*Examines them slowly, frowning.*)
How you did tick off that greengrocer. One pound fifty for a bunch of carrots, indeed. You told him, oh, yes.
(*AUNT DOLLY peers into a bag. Takes out an olive and eats it.*)
He didn't know what hit him.
(*She spits stone into sink.*)

No one fools you. You're lucky, you can do anything.
(*She takes bag of potatoes to sink, fills saucepan with cold water. Forages in drawer for knife, finds it.*)
No, it's not luck, it's character, isn't it? Character.
(*She leads him to sink, points to potatoes, puts knife in his hand.*)
What? Oh. Oh, ah –
(*He starts peeling them very slowly, stopping whenever he talks.*)
I said to Alec – you know, Alec, my friend in plastics – 'My Aunt Dolly can do anything,' I said. 'What?' he said, 'win Wimbledon?' He's silly sometimes –
(*AUNT unwraps a lettuce, gets out a salad bowl.*)
He's in Rome, by the way. On his holiday. He always used to go to Bournemouth, but he wanted a change.
(*She rootles in bags, finds onion, garlic.*)
I don't think I told you, Auntie – I've been having awful dreams. Because of this dreadful pain, I expect.
(*She bashes a garlic clove, takes off skin.*)
It's in my arm.
(*He picks up a potato.*)
There. It twitched. Did you see? All I did was pick up a potato and my arm twitched. I've been to the doctor, of course. Best to be careful.
(*She puts garlic in salad bowl, rubs it round.*)
I told him it was worse when the weather was bad. He was interested to hear that. Oh, yes. I always know when it's going to rain.
(*She chops onion very fast, very fine.*)
Auntie! Look out – you'll cut your finger. You're so reckless – you'd have been under that bus just now if I hadn't pulled you back.
(*She starts dismembering lettuce at sink.*)
I looked in at Mallards yesterday. They had a new window display – the novels of Jeffrey Archer. In my day we'd have had proper authors. Once we had ten

editions of the works of Shakespeare in the window. And
a very talented watercolour of Anne Hathaway's cottage
by Miss Armitage of accounts.

(*She washes lettuce, swirling vigorously.*)

I'm glad I took early retirement. Well, once they
introduced musak, how could I stay?

(*She looks for colander, finds it.*)

Still, I miss the place sometimes. You can't work
somewhere for five years and not miss it. And having a
job made it easier to get up in the mornings.

(*She drains lettuce vigorously.*)

I still do, of course. Get up, I mean. Can't just lie there –
have to look after Percy. It was nice of Mallards to give
him to me, but I sometimes wish they'd just handed me
the cheque and left it at that. I like to feel free – shut the
door behind me and just go. If I wanted to, that is. Well,
you never know, do you? One day, perhaps –

(*He picks up a potato, frowns at it.*)

But with a goldfish you're tied.

(*AUNT suddenly stands rigid, motionless, holding colander.*)

I'm fond of Percy. He's not like other goldfish.

(*AUNT drops colander in sink, stands rigid.*)

He's got feelings.

AUNT: Darwin's mother. Of course. It was his mother.

(*CLIVE looks at her, clutching potato.*)

Now I've noticed it's so obvious – why did I never see
before? Because I didn't bother to think, that's why.

(*CLIVE puts potato down, stares at her.*)

CLIVE: Darwin's – ? But I was telling you about –

(*AUNT picks up the three potatoes he's peeled.*)

AUNT: That all you've done? Can't wait all day –

(*She hurls all potatoes, peeled and unpeeled, into saucepan,
takes them to stove, lights the gas. Hands him beans. He sits
holding them, looking at her.*)

Here – top and tail these beans. Charles Darwin had a
most unusual brand of curiosity about everything under
the sun. I took it for granted it came from his father, or

perhaps his grandfather, Erasmus. So I never really thought about it. But just now it came to me. Quite suddenly, while I was washing the lettuce. And it's obvious. His peculiar cast of mind came from his mother. And she probably inherited it from her father, Josiah Wedgwood the Second – no slouches in the thinking stakes, those Wedgwoods –
(*Pause.*)
I'm sorry did you say something?

CLIVE: I've been talking since we came in.

AUNT: You always do. A waterfall in the background.
(*Pause.*)

CLIVE: I'm sorry I bore you.

AUNT: You don't. While you're talking I can think. I like it.
(*Silence. CLIVE toys with a bean. She looks at him, sighs, pours herself a whisky.*)
(*Conciliatory.*) How's your friend Alec?

CLIVE: In Rome. On holiday.

AUNT: Rome, eh? But he always goes to Bournemouth.

CLIVE: He wanted a change. I told you five minutes ago.

AUNT: (*Bluffing.*) So you did, how silly of me –
(*Silence. CLIVE takes the top off a bean, very slowly.*)

CLIVE: My little party was quite a success –

AUNT: (*Enthusiastic.*) Oh, good.
(*She wraps lettuce in cloth.*)

CLIVE: – considering the principal guest didn't turn up.

AUNT: No – really? How dreadfully thoughtless. People's manners nowadays are – are –
(*She drops lettuce. Stands.*)
Oh. Oh, my goodness – how perfectly frightful of me. You didn't go to a lot of trouble?

CLIVE: No, no –

AUNT: What a relief – I was afraid you'd put yourself out –

CLIVE: (*Interrupting.*) I got to Billingsgate at five, of course.
(*AUNT sits, thump.*)

For the lobsters. So I could take them home then have
time to go to Neal Street for the cheeses and on to
Notting Hill for the strawberry tart you like so much.
But I was glad to do it. I wanted you to have a nice time.

AUNT: I can't tell you how sorry I am. I not only forgot, it
never came back to my mind. Sofala Fair was running –
(*CLIVE drops a bean.*)

CLIVE: A horse. You missed my party for a horse.

AUNT: Not *a* horse. Sofala Fair. He's nothing to look at –
moves like a demented ostrich, but my word, how he
goes. And the crowd roars him home – oh, that roar,
please God I may die to the sound of it. Well, no
excuses. I was lost to the world. The horses, the shouting,
and Lumpkin saying 'Come on, Duchess, don't dilly-
dally –' as he's done any time these forty years –
(*She gets up, wraps lettuce in clean cloth.*)
Then we stopped for a little drinkie. Nothing on my
mind but cheerfulness and what a nice day we'd had.

CLIVE: It doesn't matter.

AUNT: Of course it matters. (*Fury.*) Why do you let me
walk all over you? And not only me. If I hadn't been
there you'd have bought that woebegone cauliflower the
Berwick Street greengrocer tried to unload on you – he
saw you coming. Why don't you stick up for yourself?
(*CLIVE opens his mouth.*)
Inertia, that's your trouble. Your whole life's spent sitting
around. Why don't you do something?

CLIVE: What?

AUNT: Anything – I don't know. Cross the Gobi Desert –

CLIVE: (*Puzzled.*) Why?

AUNT: Because it's there. You should never have left your
job – not that silly bookshop, your real job at Sleeman's
Bank. You've a first-rate financial mind and you've no
right to waste it. I'll never know why you left –

CLIVE: It changed. The people changed.

AUNT: Is there nothing – nothing in the world – you want
to do?

(*CLIVE considers.*)

CLIVE: Not a lot.

AUNT: How can you be so motiveless? Really, you're extraordinary –

CLIVE: Extraordinary? Me? It's you – look at you – family legend. Little Dolly at six years old telling everyone Cousin Eldred couldn't be his father's son because his eyes were the wrong colour –

AUNT: Don't know why they got upset. It was true.

CLIVE: Studying genetics at that age, I ask you –

AUNT: Why not? They've enthralled me all my life long. And so useful when I married Jack. How many racing correspondents have wives who can apply a knowledge of genetics to the breeding of horses? (*Sighs.*) I'm sorry I turned on you. It was frustration. There you are, all those years ahead –

CLIVE: For heaven's sake, I'm 54 –

AUNT: That's right. All those years and nothing to do with them. And here I am, time shortening as we talk – you can see the bugger rushing by. And when I die who will remember Jack?

(*She goes to bookcase, takes out thick book, hands it to CLIVE.*)

Here. Diary of my life with him – all his jokes. Take it. Read it. Then you'll see why he should be a household name. I asked my old college to found a chair on the breeding of horses in his memory – well, what could be more instructive for the young? Come back with half a million, they said, and we'll talk turkey.

CLIVE: Does it matter so much?

AUNT: Yes.

CLIVE: Why?

AUNT: There are reasons.

(*He opens his mouth, she glares at him.*)

Reasons.

(*She starts chopping parsley furiously.*)

So now – at my age – I've got to make half a million.

CLIVE: Don't be silly. You can't.

AUNT: Can't? Defeatist nonsense.

(*She stops chopping parsley, glares at him.*)

You look the image of my brother sitting there. But you're not like him. He had fire.

(*Silence. CLIVE starts chopping beans, very slowly.*)

I shouldn't have said that. Unforgiveable.

(*CLIVE does one bean, very slowly. Starts whistling 'Annie Laurie'. AUNT looks at him, frowns, starts trying to attract his attention. He goes on whistling 'Annie Laurie'.*)

That dreadful woman from the Old Folk's Welfare came ringing at the door yesterday. I knew it was her. Knew if I didn't answer she'd start peering through the letterbox. But I was a match for her. Got my plant spray –

(*She picks up plant spray, heads for the door. CLIVE concentrates on beans.*)

Clive. Pay attention.

(*He looks up, reluctantly; stops whistling.*)

I tiptoe to the door – and freeze.

(*He is hooked in spite of himself.*)

I wait. Ring ring she goes again. I tense – the SAS about to jump terrorists. Slowly the flap of the letterbox goes up – but I hold my fire. It opens wider – zam – I get her. Right between the eyes.

(*CLIVE begins to laugh.*)

I fling open the door and there she is, full length on the floor. 'No need to grovel, Miss Um,' I said. 'A curtsy would have sufficed.'

CLIVE: You always know how to win a person back – just by making him laugh.

AUNT: Call that nothing?

CLIVE: No. You've won. As usual. Unfairly. As usual.

AUNT: I'm sorry. I keep forgetting how thin-skinned you are. I never saw much of you until Jack died, and that's –

(*She stops.*)

– under two years. Good grief. Is that all? Seems like eternity, damn him. How dare he turn his toes up and pop off without a by-your-leave? My bed's cold, my feet are cold, and I've no one to talk to.

CLIVE: I'm sure Uncle Jack didn't mean to die.

AUNT: They all do it. When I read *The Times* and there's no one I know in the death column I shout 'Well done – you've all made it through the night –' and if I'm not in it I have a double brandy. Look at your mother, popping off like that –

CLIVE: Mother couldn't help dying.

AUNT: Oh, stop making excuses for everyone –
(*Police sirens outside; CLIVE goes to window, shudders.*)

CLIVE: I wish you'd move, Auntie. Soho's not safe. I could find you a nice cottage in the country –

AUNT: (*Scorn.*) Country? Soho suits me. Canaletto lived just round the corner painting away like a little demon, and if it was good enough for him it's good enough for me. Country, indeed. I'm far too busy. Got to make half a million, keep out of the clutches of the cosy home, and stay alive. This is no time to sing along with the *Missa Solemnis.* And hurry up with those beans – got a busy afternoon ahead –

CLIVE: What's up?

AUNT: Doing a flit. Quick quick round the corner, licketty split, no forwarding address. Ha. That'll fox 'em.

CLIVE: (*Goggling.*) Who? Fox who?

AUNT: I just told you, your memory's going – why don't you keep active like me? The Old Folks' Welfare. They're a menace – skulking there waiting to pounce. 'Come along, Dolly dear, we've been waiting for you –' clang, the door slams to, and they've got you – fiendish laughter on the other side.

CLIVE: Oh, nonsense –

AUNT: They got my friend Aggie. (*Pause.*) I won't think about her. (*Pause.*) No. I won't.
(*She stops; stands. Gives a shiver, speaks briskly.*)
Well. End of our Saturday shopping if they collar me –

CLIVE: Have a nice time, don't we?

AUNT: Clive –

CLIVE: I look forward to it all week –

AUNT: Clive!

(*He looks at her, surprised. Silence.*)

Don't let them lock me up. (*Pause.*) I don't want to die diminished.

CLIVE: (*Indignant.*) Of course I won't let them.

AUNT: Silly of me, of course you won't. Anyhow, they can't catch me now. Thought they might lie in wait for me at the bank – do a dawn swoop. So I've drawn out every penny.

(*She turns the gas up under the potatoes.*)

£40,000. Should see me out.

CLIVE: Forty – but what have you done with it? Where – ? Oh, my God, it's here – under the mattress – in the ice box – how could you be so silly? Where is it?

(*She inspects potatoes.*)

AUNT: I gave it to Lumpkin.

CLIVE: Lumpkin? Second time you've mentioned him. Who is he?

AUNT: One of my oldest friends.

CLIVE: Then why don't I know him?

AUNT: I don't mix my worlds. (*Pause.*) He's a bookie.

CLIVE: A bookie? You've given your money to a bookie?

AUNT: Not *a* bookie. Lumpkin. Jack said he'd go through a jungle with Lumpkin and that's good enough for me.

(*CLIVE splutters, horrified.*)

Lumpkin is now my bank. Much more fun than that dreary high street place. He brings the cash, we have a drink and a nice chat.

CLIVE: Auntie – you can't. I'm sure he's a first-rate bookie, but –

AUNT: Nothing of the kind. He just inherited the family business. Bores him stiff. Left to himself he'd sit around reading *Treasure Island.* He dotes on that book, gets to the end and goes back to page one, don't know why he bothers when he knows it by heart.

(*She notices CLIVE goggling at her.*)

Being my bank gives him an interest. His worshipped his brother Tad and my Jack – all he ever wanted was to trundle along in their wake, happy as a sandboy. So of course they went and died, and now poor Lumpkin has an empty heart.

(*She takes a chocolate biscuit.*)

Of course he drives me mad sometimes. Silly old fool, refusing to lay my money out on Clouds of Glory –

(*CLIVE sits, horrified.*)

The Gold Cup's five months away and that horse is going to win it – think of the odds Lumpkin would get now. But he says as my bank he feels responsible, old twerp –

CLIVE: Auntie. I want to meet him.

AUNT: What's the point? He hasn't the first idea about shopping. Can't see Lumpkin comparing the price of carrots. Round the corner for fish and chips or a sausage washed down with whisky for him – you'd have nothing in common.

(*Helps herself to another biscuit.*)

Besides – it doesn't do to mix worlds. Embarrasses people. We're gypsies, Lumpkin and I. Vagabonds. And you're not. Don't try to join the vagabonds. You'd be very unhappy.

(*Silence. She takes another biscuit.*)

CLIVE: That's your third chocolate biscuit.

AUNT: Really? Amazing how they slip down with the whisky.

(*CLIVE tops and tails a bean, very slowly. Silence.*)

CLIVE: What would I do in the Gobi Desert? If I knew how find it? Ride a camel? Sand up my nostrils, no thank you –

(*Doorbell. AUNT stiffens.*)

AUNT: (*Whispers.*) It's her.

(*CLIVE goes to answer the door, she pulls him back. Silence. Doorbell goes again.*)

KATE: (*Off.*) Professor Delaney – I'm Kate Hammond. Your new social worker.

AUNT: New who wants new what's this?

KATE: (*Off.*) You've given poor Dawn a breakdown squirting her through the letter box. She's lying in a darkened room under sedation.

(*AUNT grins.*)

(*Off.*) No need to smile.

AUNT: (*Hisses to CLIVE.*) She's psychic.

KATE: (*Off.*) You're thinking I'm psychic. I'm not. But I've got your measure.

(*Noise of letterbox being raised. AUNT and CLIVE dive behind sofa.*)

I think you're hiding behind the sofa.

(*They crouch lower.*)

But for all I know you've had a fall and you're lying there helpless. So I'm coming in.

AUNT: Open the door – quick – get rid of her –

(*She dives for the bedroom and shuts the door. CLIVE opens door; KATE comes bursting in. She is 25ish, good-looking, not at all pretty. Fierce, uncompromising, with a lot of energy that doesn't know where it's going. Silence. She looks round the room.*)

KATE: Where is she?

CLIVE: She's got a headache. She's lying down. (*Pause.*) I'm Clive Warren – her nephew.

KATE: (*Amazed.*) You? But she's a killer. And you look so – so –

CLIVE: (*Menacing.*) Well? Go on – useless – unmotivated –

KATE: No. Mild. Just – mild. Hey – something's boiling –

CLIVE: Oh – the potatoes –

(*He finds fork to prod them. KATE brushes him to one side, takes fork.*)

KATE: Let me.

(*She prods potatoes. CLIVE opens his mouth to protest, she doesn't notice. He tries to get fork back, she brushes him aside.*)
I'll do it – colander?
(*She holds out hand for the colander. CLIVE doesn't move. She smiles at him, friendly.*)
No trouble. I like helping people.
(*CLIVE passes the colander, hypnotised. She drains potatoes, tastes one, hurls them into trash can. CLIVE looks at can, at her.*)

CLIVE: My potatoes –

KATE: Soggy. Yuk.

CLIVE: My potatoes.

KATE: And you forgot the salt.
(*She puts colander in sink. Looks at him.*)
You look shell-shocked. I suppose she's done a hatchet job on you. Like she did on Dawn.
(*CLIVE crumples.*)

CLIVE: She didn't mean to –

KATE: She did. She's old, she's frightened, so she lashes out. If we looked after her she'd be nicer because she'd feel safe – part of one big happy family.

CLIVE: What's happy about families?

KATE: Answer to everything. Or so I'm told –
(*CLIVE opens his mouth to speak, but she goes on.*)
I never had one. My parents were killed in a car crash and I was brought up by Uncle Giles and Aunt Deborah. In Morpeth. He was a bank manager, collected pottery busts of Napoleon, she wore gloves to do the shopping and there wasn't a book in the house –
(*CLIVE again tries to speak, but she goes on.*)
I tell a lie. There was a set of Shakespeare in a glass case. I started *Hamlet*, but Aunt Deborah put a plastic cover on him, told me to wash my hands first and not to open him too wide or I'd break his spine. So I put him back and she shut the glass case to keep out the dust. That put me off and I've never read him – have you?
(*CLIVE opens his mouth; can't get a word in.*)

Well, I got away from Morpeth, and –
(*CLIVE holds his head, sways slightly, clutches table.*)
You all right?
CLIVE: (*Faintly.*) Fine – fine –
KATE: I've taken first aid – want me to check your heart?
CLIVE: (*Shuddering.*) No – I'm fine –
KATE: Where was I? Oh, yes. I got away. London. New life.
Saw this job in the *Evening Standard* – social work, train
as you go – and I thought – yes. Then I could help
people like my history teacher in Morpeth helped me.
Miss Wilkins. I'd never met anyone truly kind before,
and oh, the difference she made. Because she was good, I
suppose. I want to be like her.
(*CLIVE looks bemused; she glares at him.*)
Well? Is it so strange to want to be good?
(*CLIVE opens his mouth but she goes on.*)
So I've dedicated my life to social work why are you
looking like that?
CLIVE: Well – I can see you leading a cavalry charge –
thundering into battle. But an ordinary routine job? No.
There's just too much of you for everyday life.
(*She crumples, utterly.*)
What have I said?
KATE: Daniel's very words when he walked out on me last
week. My boyfriend Daniel. Well. Was my boyfriend.
'There's too much of you, Kate, for everyday life.' But
he'd said he loved me – said it again and again. So I
believed him, of course I did. You have to believe what
people say or where are you? What's life without trust,
tell me that.
(*Glares at CLIVE, who opens his mouth, but she goes on.*)
And everything was going so well. (*Sighs.*) 'Love seemed
easy at first, but soon snags appeared.' The poet Hafiz
said that. Knew his onions, didn't he?
(*CLIVE opens his mouth, but she goes on.*)
Same with jobs. They start well, everyone's pleased to
see me – 'What a help you are, Kate, how did we ever

manage without you?' Suddenly the world blows up and it's 'Goodbye, Miss Hammond –'

(*Glares at CLIVE.*)

What's wrong with them all?

CLIVE: Them? It's you. Take a look at yourself. You roar in like a force nine gale, commandeer the kitchen, pulp the potatoes, thunder through your childhood, charge full-throttle through your love life – all without drawing breath. And I feel like those potatoes you trashed. They never knew what hit them and neither do I. You frighten people off, that's what you do.

(*Silence. She looks at him, puzzled.*)

KATE: Why?

CLIVE: (*Exasperated.*) I just told you – (*Pause.*) Now I've upset you –

KATE: No. No, not at all. Upset, good heavens.

(*Silence. She frowns.*)

Please try and stick to the point. We're not here to talk about me, we're here to decide about your Aunt. She's not safe on her own, you know. She's practically blind.

CLIVE: Nonsense – short-sighted.

KATE: Blind. Her oculist sent us a report – for her own protection. She must live in a thick fog –

CLIVE: (*Horror.*) Oh, my God. She nearly did go under that bus. (*Pause.*) And I thought she was invincible.

KATE: No. She's old. Very old. (*Pause.*) Hand her over to us. We'll look after her.

CLIVE: Betray her? Of course I won't.

KATE: But she must get so tired – and there's this flat to clean –

CLIVE: Oh, I do that. Of course. Look at the floor – spotless.

(*She looks at the floor, at him.*)

And this table – it's lovely rosewood, but she will bang her whisky glass down on it. I have quite a fight to get the stains out –

(*She looks at table, at him.*)

KATE: How kind you are. Why, you're like Miss Wilkins.
(*Pause.*) Look, we both want what's best for her –
CLIVE: You're right. Let's work it out together.
(*He goes to kettle, puts in water, puts it on.*)
Tea?
(*She looks pleased. Sits, looks around. Sees diary; picks it up.*)
KATE: What's this?
CLIVE: Uncle Jack's diary. Have a look –
(*She starts reading, he gets out mugs. She notices mugs, puts down diary, goes to cupboard he got them from, finds two china cups and saucers, puts mugs back in cupboard. CLIVE sees cups, looks irritated. She picks up diary again.*)
KATE: Knew she'd have proper china. Tea tastes foul in mugs.
(*She starts reading. Laughs.*)
Why, it's funny, it's very funny –
(*She notices he's got tea bags out. Puts down diary with a sigh, goes to cupboard, finds tin of tea, opens it.*)
Lapsang Suchong. Knows what's what, doesn't she?
(*CLIVE shovels tea into teapot in a fury. She grabs it from him, puts tea back into tin.*)
Stop! You haven't warmed the pot.
(*He tries to get teapot back, she hangs on to it.*)
Brings out the flavour. Thought everyone knew that.
(*She fills pot with hot water. He stands, looks at her.*)
Don't thank me. I like helping people –
CLIVE: Kate. How long were you and Daniel together?
KATE: (*Puzzled.*) Three months. Two days. Why?
CLIVE: (*Aghast.*) Three months! The man's a hero – how did he stand it? He deserves a medal. Look, I can see you're very nice, really, but you're so tactless – well, intolerable – yes, intolerable, that's the word – you'd drive anyone mad. Of course he left you, who wouldn't?
(*She looks at him, stunned, uncomprehending.*)
KATE: Oh! How dare you pretend to be like Miss Wilkins – what cheek. You're nothing like. I thought you were so

nice, but you're horrid – unkind and horrid. Well I certainly won't help you any more – and if you choke on your foul tea bags and your soggy potatoes I'll just laugh –

(*She storms out.*)

CLIVE: What on earth's the matter? Where are you going? You can't come on like the charge of the Light Brigade then bolt like a startled rabbit – come back – (*Shouts.*) Kettle's boiling –

(*AUNT comes bursting in, shoots over to chest of drawers, starts collecting things.*)

AUNT: I'm moving this minute. Started packing the moment I heard that voice – sounded like my old governess –

CLIVE: Auntie –

AUNT: – used to dose us with laudanum to keep us quiet –

CLIVE: Auntie –

(*He stands about four feet away; holds up one hand.*)

How many fingers?

(*Pause.*)

AUNT: Boring question.

CLIVE: How many?

AUNT: Several.

(*He holds hand in front of her nose.*)

Three, of course. Could see all along. Just fooling.

(*She grabs things she's collected. Heads for bedroom carrying them.*)

CLIVE: You should never go out on your own – one day you'll be scraped off the street –

AUNT: (*Off.*) Have to leave something to providence –

(*She comes back.*)

– what it's there for.

CLIVE: You're my responsibility.

AUNT: What? When you can't cope with a goldfish?

(*She burrows in chest of drawers.*)

I've lived free and I'll die free. If Jack were alive he'd back me. And it's him I'm answerable to. And God, I suppose, if he exists. I have doubts about him. But if he does exist he'll agree with Jack – be a fool not to, Jack's always right.

CLIVE: But you're in danger –

AUNT: Who isn't? World's a jungle. If you feel you shouldn't help me, I don't want to come between you and your conscience. But in that case leave me to find my own way. And don't come looking.

CLIVE: No choice, have I? That's blackmail.

AUNT: (*Smug.*) Yes, isn't it?
(*She takes things into bedroom, comes out, gets black plastic bag, holds it open.*)
Come on – empty the fridge –
(*CLIVE shovels everything in, does up plastic bag, takes it, puts it outside the front door, comes back.*)
Cases. In my room.
(*He goes, comes back staggering under two enormous cases.*)

CLIVE: Ow – my shoulder –
(*He puts cases down, rubs shoulder.*)
The doctor said –

AUNT: Come along, don't dawdle.
(*He picks up cases. Agony. Looks at diary, tries to pick it up, fails, leaves it.*)
I always believe in travelling light.
(*He follows her out.*)

Scene Two

Three months later; the same room. AUNT bursts in, not diminished but distracted. CLIVE trails in after her. She slams the door and leans against it, panting.

AUNT: You're sure we weren't followed?

CLIVE: Why should anyone?
(*She starts going through drawers. CLIVE goes to table, runs his finger through the dust. Goes at once for duster, polish, polishing cloth. Starts working on table. AUNT increasingly*

frantic as she goes through drawers. CLIVE watches her as he works.)

That's no way to find things.

(*She hurls things about.*)

No, you'll never find anything like that –

(*She looks round the room. She's shaking.*)

Look at the state you're in – you're not yourself. Moving three times in three months – my back will never be the same. The doctor says I'm my own worst enemy.

(*He stops polishing.*)

What was wrong with 110b Old Compton Street? Perfectly good flat. But there you go, moonlight flit after two weeks. Shepherds' Market, five weeks, a record that was – Lexington Street, lying low, diving for cover – just because you think poor Kate's on your heels.

(*He watches AUNT burrowing through drawers.*)

No, you'll never find anything like that –

(*AUNT slams drawer to, rounds on him.*)

AUNT: Shut up and let me get on.

(*She goes back to tearing the drawers apart.*)

CLIVE: Well. Sorry I spoke.

(*He polishes in a miffed manner.*)

All this fuss for a ring –

AUNT: Jack's ring, you fool, Jack's ring. There's no luck without it. How could I have forgotten it?

(*She tries more drawers. He watches her.*)

CLIVE: I always think it's best to be tidy. A place for everything and everything in its place. Then you can find things when you want them.

(*She tries another drawer.*)

I always think –

AUNT: *Shut up.*

(*She takes a deep breath.*)

I'm sorry. But please stop driving me mad. Leave me to –

(*She stops, motionless. Looks in drawer, very slowly takes out ring. Silence. She sits with a thump. Beams at ring.*)

CLIVE: Satisfied?

(*AUNT's beam gradually fades. She sits, looking at ring.*)

AUNT: Oh, lord. What a fool I am. What a fool.

(*Silence.*)

Did I think it would bring him back? It's just a ring and he's dead.

(*She sits, totally crumpled. CLIVE puts a hand on her shoulder. Slowly she gets up, heads for door.*)

Fool's errand – what an old fool I am. Come on, let's go –

(*CLIVE sits, suddenly.*)

What's the matter?

CLIVE: Nothing – I'm all right –

AUNT: You've never said that in your life, you must be ill –

(*She goes over, peers at him.*)

Good heavens –

(*Goes to cupboard, pours him large brandy.*)

Here – brandy.

CLIVE: Just felt a bit faint. I can't sleep, you see – well, I worry all the time – have you fallen under a lorry – set fire to yourself. And if I doze off, the nightmares –

(*AUNT sits, slowly. Silence.*)

AUNT: Oh, my. Oh, my word. I had no idea.

CLIVE: Talk to Kate – oh, don't look like that, she's very nice – got a bit of a temper but she's sorry afterwards. I ring her when I'm so worried I don't know what to do. Daresay Uncle Jack would have gone through a jungle with her. She'd certainly scare the tigers.

(*She sits, twisting her ring.*)

Please. Don't look like you've been betrayed. She won't lock you up – she's resourceful, she'll think of something. (*Pause.*) She comes from Morpeth.

(*Silence.*)

AUNT: (*Snarls.*) Go on. Ring her.

(*CLIVE dives for telephone.*)

CLIVE: You won't be sorry, she'll – Kate, I'm at my Aunt's
flat – can you come now? She wants to see you –
(*He rings off.*)
She'll be here in half an hour. Doesn't hang about, oh no.
She's like you – decisive.
AUNT: I can't face that woman without a drink, but I
finished the whisky. Could you –
CLIVE: Of course. I'll nip round the corner and get some.
AUNT: (*Dubious.*) Thank you –
(*CLIVE stops on his way to the door.*)
Berry Brothers have a wonderful Irish malt –
CLIVE: But they're half a mile away –
AUNT: You're right – just go round the corner –
(*CLIVE heads for door again.*)
I thought as it was my last drink in this flat, but no – it's
too far. And the hill up St James's on the way back – no,
go round the corner – get anything – what does it
matter?
CLIVE: Of course I'll get your malt.
AUNT: No, no – too much trouble –
CLIVE: Rubbish. I'll be quick as I can –
(*He goes. She gets up.*)
AUNT: Twenty minutes' grace –
(*She stands, looking at ring.*)
Damn you, Jack. Help me through the jungle.

Scene Three

Same room, half an hour later. CLIVE comes in, holding bottle.

CLIVE: Auntie! I'm back –
(*He puts bottle on table, gets out three glasses.*)
Let's have a drink now – before she gets here.
(*He examines the glasses, shudders. Takes them to sink, washes
them.*)
You two will get on like a house on fire. You're both such
fighters. (*Sighs.*) Not like me.

(*Dries glasses, polishes.*)

I'm not what you'd like me to be, I know. I'm sorry. But I can't change. You can only be what you are.

(*Breathes on glasses, polishes hard. Sound of doorbell. He shouts.*)

She's here, Auntie –

(*Goes to door, lets in KATE, who looks upset.*)

KATE: You've worn her down.

CLIVE: I like that. Who said she should be safe in a home?

KATE: I didn't know what I was talking about. I'd never been inside one. (*Shivers.*) Well, now I have – part of my training. And yes, they're safe. And they'd break her spirit in days. (*Pause.*) I don't want her to die diminished. (*Silence. She picks up diary, opens it. CLIVE stands, motionless, then goes to the bottle; pours three whiskies, violent.*) Have you read the diary yet?

CLIVE: (*Savage.*) No – you read it – take it – find a publisher –

(*She looks at him, surprised. Shrugs. Puts diary in her holdall; CLIVE downs whisky in one.*)

Let's get it over. Auntie!

(*Pause.*)

Aunt Dolly!

(*He goes to bedroom door. Opens it. Rushes in. Comes out, distraught.*)

She's not there –

(*He runs about the flat, looking in corners where she couldn't possibly be. KATE picks up whisky, beams.*)

But she sent me to get whisky so we could have a drink –

(*Silence.*)

She lied. (*Disbelieving.*) She lied to me.

KATE: Never mind. She's got away –

CLIVE: (*Fury.*) But she's in danger – you said so yourself –

KATE: So what? She's free.

CLIVE: (*Fury.*) How can you be so uncaring?

KATE: She'll die undiminished. Nothing else matters.

(*Doorbell goes. CLIVE heads for door.*)

CLIVE: Ah! She just went out and forgot her keys – again –
(*He opens door.*)
Well, welcome back –
(*He stops. Silence. GWYNNE comes in, mild. He is a quiet, watchful man with a pronounced Welsh accent. He is smiling in a friendly, almost conspiratorial, manner.*)

GWYNNE: Voices upraised in argument. On such a lovely day.
(*He hands CLIVE his card. CLIVE looks at it, at him.*)

CLIVE: Detective Sergeant Gwynne –
(*KATE comes, looks at card. They both look at GWYNNE, who smiles. Silence.*)
My aunt – something's happened –
(*GWYNNE comes in, looks around.*)

GWYNNE: A nice light room, no dark corners –

CLIVE: She's gone under a bus –

GWYNNE: Are all the rooms as light, I wonder?
(*He moves very fast, very quiet, to bathroom, bedroom. Comes back.*)
No dark corners anywhere. A very desirable residence.
(*He goes to bookshelves.*)
Books, yes indeed. Books –
(*He takes one from shelves.*)
Genetic Movements in Primitive Societies, by Professor Dorothea Delaney. And a photograph of the author on the cover.
(*He holds it up.*)
A good likeness?

CLIVE: Yes, very – oh, come on, Sergeant – what's happened?
(*Briskly GWYNNE sets two chairs; indicates them. CLIVE and KATE sit; CLIVE moves one of the chairs. GWYNNE puts it back.*)
But the sun's in my eyes –

GWYNNE: A rare occurrence in this country, sir. You should be grateful.

(He sits behind desk, facing them. They wriggle.)
You are upset. Why?
He sits back, hands folded, motionless. Watches, listens. The more he says nothing the more they talk.)

CLIVE: I thought you'd come to say my aunt had gone under a bus.
(He waits for some response; none comes.)
She's very short-sighted – I didn't realise how bad her eyes had got. How was I to know, she always pretended she was fine.
(GWYNNE picks up a silver object from the table.)
All right, I should have noticed. Well I didn't. I just didn't. Yes, I was heedless and thoughtless, why don't you say something?
(GWYNNE examines object, thorough, meticulous. Silence.)

KATE: I'm Professor Delaney's social worker, Kate Hammond.
(GWYNNE goes on examining object, puzzled, still smiling.)
She's running away from me. Because I thought she should be in a home for her own good. I was wrong. I hounded the poor old thing – so to her I was the enemy – no humanity, no compassion.
(She is watching GWYNNE anxiously, but he is oblivious. Silence.)

CLIVE: *(Fury.)* We're talking to you –
(GWYNNE holds up object.)

GWYNNE: What is this?

CLIVE: A marrow scoop.

GWYNNE: A marrow scoop.
(Examines it again, closely. Puts it down, smiling apologetically.)
It is important in my profession to know the use of things, their nature. You never know when you may need such knowledge. It can make the difference between losing a man –
(Picks up scoop again.)
– or nailing him.

CLIVE: (*Fury.*) What are you doing here? You sit playing
    with that thing, don't listen to a word –

GWYNNE: Don't listen, Mr Warren?
    (*He stops smiling, speaks very fast, no intonation.*)
    I thought you'd come to say my aunt had gone under a
    bus. She's very short-sighted – I didn't realise how bad
    her eyes had got. How was I to know, she always
    pretended she was fine. All right, I should have noticed.
    Well I didn't. I just didn't. Yes, I was heedless and
    thoughtless why don't you say something? We're talking
    to you –
    (*Pause.*)
    I listen, Mr Warren. Oh, yes.
    (*Silence. He looks at them.*)
    Now. Let us begin. You last saw your Aunt – ?

CLIVE: An hour ago. She sent me to buy whisky. When I
    came back she'd gone.

GWYNNE: Did you see her, Miss Hammond?

KATE: She left before I got here.

GWYNNE: So no one but you has seen her, Mr Warren.
    Oh, dear. (*Sighs.*) You are asking yourself why I am here.
    There are three reasons. First, we've had enquiries. You
    say she was here an hour ago. I find that hard to credit.
    No one in this building has seen her for three months.

CLIVE: She hasn't been here, that's why.

GWYNNE: But this afternoon she was. (*Pause.*) Where has
    she been?

CLIVE: Moving from flat to flat.

GWYNNE: Wanderlust is a rare affliction in the old.

CLIVE: She's been on the run – she thought Kate would
    force her into a home. And no one else has seen her
    because she was hiding.

GWYNNE: From Miss Hammond?

KATE: Yes. I'm sorry.

GWYNNE: (*To CLIVE.*) You and the old lady were close?

CLIVE: Very.

GWYNNE: So you know she recently made a will.

CLIVE: Know? I forced her to – practically had to write it myself –

GWYNNE: You are her heir.

CLIVE: She told me.

GWYNNE: And you made her write a will.

CLIVE: Of course. Die intestate and the Income Tax gets every penny. I told her to leave her money to a hospital for performing fleas – whatever – as long as she made a will. In the end she left it all to to me. Silly, I told her I didn't want anything – I've got enough. (*Pause.*) Why are you smiling?

GWYNNE: Was I? Forgive me.

CLIVE: Why are you reading her will when she's alive?

GWYNNE: The second reason I'm here. Her bank rang us because they were worried. They hadn't heard from the old lady for months – they said she'd disappeared. But just before she went off – if that is what happened – she withdrew every penny she had. £40,000. In cash.

CLIVE: That's right.

GWYNNE: You knew.

CLIVE: She told me. Naturally.

GWYNNE: Because of you being so close, yes, of course. (*Pause.*) Where is the money, I wonder?

CLIVE: She gave it to Lumpkin.

(*GWYNNE looks at him.*)

Her oldest friend. She asked him to be her bank.

GWYNNE: Lumpkin. A rare name. (*Pause.*) He has a profession?

CLIVE: He's a bookie.

GWYNNE: A bookie. Your aunt asked a bookie to act as her bank. What an unusual old lady she is turning out to be.

KATE: She's an old monster – impossible –

GWYNNE: A strange thing to say about a poor old woman. But perhaps your social work is only skin deep. Perhaps you don't care about the sick, the homeless –

KATE: How can you say that? How can you think it? I do care, I do. How can anyone not? Every time I see some poor drug-ridden waif in a Soho gutter I think of his mother and the dreams she had for him, the great things he'd do – conquer the world, perhaps? How mothers think, isn't it? How –
(*Her voice dies away. Silence.*)
Oh, hell.

GWYNNE: Thank you, Miss Hammond. Now. Mr Lumpkin's address?

CLIVE: How should I know? I've never met him.

GWYNNE: But he was your Aunt's oldest friend. And you and she were so close.

CLIVE: She has a lot of worlds. She doesn't mix them.

GWYNNE: A lot of worlds. Well, well. We generally find with old people one world is all they can cope with. If that. We worry when an old person goes missing. (*Pause.*) You must be worried about your Aunt.

CLIVE: I was. Until I realised she'd given me the slip so she could disappear. She'll be heading for some race course, alive and well and drinking some poor sod under the table.

GWYNNE: We appear to be discussing two different people. You have in mind a wild, flighty old party up to no good.

CLIVE: Thought you hadn't met her.
(*GWYNNE picks up AUNT's book, reads blurb on back cover.*)

GWYNNE: 'Professor Delaney was at one time a highly respected don at Girton, the first woman to hold a chair in genetics. Her work on blood-strains in isolated areas of the Pennines is unlikely to be surpassed in the next fifty years.'
(*He puts down book.*)
Well, think of that. A great scholar. A fine, austere mind. But you ask me to believe this elderly pillar of the learned world goes hopping from race course to race

course handing enormous sums to a bookie. In between
double whiskies.

CLIVE: Not *a* bookie. Lumpkin.

GWYNNE: I know that world. There is no Lumpkin.

CLIVE: There is. She said so.

GWYNNE: Describe him.

(*Pause. CLIVE frowns.*)

CLIVE: Knows *Treasure Island* by heart. (*Pause.*) Don't look
at me like that – it's what she said.

GWYNNE: Oh, what a tangled web we weave, when first we
practise to deceive.

(*CLIVE jumps up, fury.*)

CLIVE: That's enough. You sit there smiling –

GWYNNE: Smiling?

(*Silence.*)

Look again.

(*CLIVE looks. GWYNNE indicates chair. CLIVE sits,
slowly.*)

My job is to seek truth. Its pursuit is not only my job but
my passion. But to find it I have to sift through lies.
Everyone lies to the police – not always intentionally.
Take Miss Hammond. Does she care about the homeless?
Or was she thinking of her own loneliness in a great
uncaring city? People's words are so seldom what they
seem.

(*He pauses, frowns.*)

And you, Mr Warren. You told me you did not want
money. I smiled. I am familiar with human nature, its
double dealing, its profound darkness. Its study is my
professional life. I watch, I listen, I sift. And the training
of years tells me a man who says he doesn't want money
is lying, so he's a liar, so what else will he lie about?
Take this Lumpkin, this bookie without a name, so
beguiling that old women flock to him with their money
– you ask me to believe in him?

(*CLIVE opens his mouth, but GWYNNE over-rides him.*)

Until the lies are sifted I am in the dark. And I hate the dark. Frightened of it, to be honest. At the best of times my rest is uneasy. My wife tells me I talk in my sleep – a mindless babble. But when I'm on a case I have insomnia. Silly, isn't it? How childish we all are. (*Shakes his head, smiles.*)

And as I lie watchful in the menacing dark, I think of murder. I was brought up Chapel, and taught to respect life as God-given. So I hate murder, you see. And murderers – sir. Above all I hate murderers who kill old women for their money – sir.

(*CLIVE goggles, speechless.*)

You look as if you would not say boo to a goose. No one would pick you as a man likely to murder his poor old Auntie in cold blood. But there's no art to find the mind's construction in the face. (*Pause.*) Is there, sir?

KATE: He loves his Aunt –

GWYNNE: You are so sure what he says is true. You must know him very well.

KATE: No, this is only the second time we've met –

GWYNNE: My. How your acquaintance has burgeoned.

(*He turns to CLIVE.*)

Where is the dear old lady? Where is her body?

CLIVE: (*Fury.*) You're very stupid. Why should I kill the only person in the world who makes me laugh?

(*He gets up.*)

I've had enough of this foolishness. I'm going home.

GWYNNE: Going already? When we're getting on so comfortably?

CLIVE: Can you keep me here?

GWYNNE: No.

CLIVE: Then I'm going.

(*He heads for door. KATE follows him, turns at door.*)

KATE: Think you can read everyone's heart, don't you? Sitting there playing God. God, indeed – seedy Jesuit, that's you –

(She follows CLIVE out. Left alone, GWYNNE stays sitting in the chair. Picks up marrow scoop, looks at it. Directs it with sudden violence at his eye. Observes it. Shakes his head. Puts it down tidily. Sits silent, patient, hands folded, waiting. Sound of uproar below. He doesn't move a muscle, sits silent, patient, waiting.

CLIVE and KATE burst in, CLIVE dishevelled and breathless.)

GWYNNE: So you've met the third reason I am here. Our local Italians. They're all so fond of your Auntie. And for some reason they hold you responsible for her disappearance. Like us, they have their spies. One of them must have spotted you.

(He gets up, goes to window.)

My word. Look out there and what breeding you do see – scions of the great families from the hot-blooded south. Why, half of Sicily is waiting for a word with you. Dear me, what lineage those lads have got.

(He turns to CLIVE.)

Sit down.

(CLIVE hovers.)

Sit.

(CLIVE and KATE both sit.)

Let us put the information together, piece by piece. Oh, I do love information. Meat and drink to me, it is, and sex as well. Put the fragments together and light is born. We cannot see it yet, the darkness is absolute. Let us seek it together – seek and ye shall find. *(Pause.)* I will have light.

Scene Four

Five weeks later. CLIVE and KATE have just arrived in AUNT's flat. CLIVE picks up large pile of letters on floor.

KATE: I told you, didn't I? I said there was no point in
      coming. She's not here and she hasn't been back. I told
      you –

CLIVE: All right, I was wrong, no need to rub it in. (*Snarls.*)
      I've had enough. Five weeks and no sign of her. Five
      weeks of being dragged into the police station and
      questioned – five weeks of Sergeant Gwynne –
      (*He opens a letter; frowns.*)
      'You have already won one of the following splendid
      prizes – a BMW, a holiday for two in the fabulous
      Bahamas, the fitted kitchen of your dreams, a leather
      bookmark –' A leather bookmark, that's nice.
      (*KATE grabs the letters and starts going through them, fast.*)
      Wonder if you can choose the colour?
      (*KATE throws down letters.*)

KATE: Nothing. Oh, where can she be?

CLIVE: (*Cross.*) How do I know? Gone with the vagabonds,
      most like – over the hills and far away.

KATE: Vagabonds?

CLIVE: A select company I can never join, because they're
      carefree and light of heart. Laughing as they down the
      whisky and tirra lirra by the river blithely sang Sir
      Lancelot. No place for me, she was right.

KATE: She said that?

CLIVE: She didn't mean to hurt.

KATE: She did. Like when she told you to head for the
      Gobi Desert. She knows just how to put the boot in –

CLIVE: (*Quiet.*) No –

KATE: Why don't you look? Before her husband died she
      never bothered with you, did she? (*Pause.*) Did she?

CLIVE: Oh, dear – just look at my table – what a state it's
      in –
      (*He goes to drawer, gets duster, polishing cloth.*)

KATE: You do everything for her –
      (*CLIVE dusts resolutely.*)
      – she takes your company when she feels like it and you
      make yourself scarce when she doesn't. She's very lucky

to have such a kind nephew and she doesn't appreciate
you a bit – she's a card-carrying monster –
(*Silence. CLIVE dusts, looks miserable.*)
I'm sorry. Sorry. I shouldn't have said that. But I got the
sack last week and I suppose I'm a bit sour.

CLIVE: Oh. Oh, dear. (*Pause.*) Did you tell them how to
run a home for old people?

KATE: No – I didn't do anything. It's just like always.
(*Pause.*) I was cross when you said I frightened people off
– thought you were being stupid. But now I see you may
be right. Clever of you.
(*She looks at him admiringly.*)
You must be very perceptive. Perhaps you are like Miss
Wilkins, after all. So you'll be able to help me, tell me
where I go wrong –
(*CLIVE opens his mouth in horror, but she goes on.*)
By the way, I read the diary. It's very funny, I laughed
and laughed. So having time on my hands I've been
looking for a publisher. Weird lot. Most of them wouldn't
even see me. But I think I've found one. Mr Ben Rumble
– of Wortledge and Rumble – said he liked it – gave me
a letter for your Aunt.

CLIVE: (*Goggling.*) But they're the grandest publisher in
London – how on earth did you get in?

KATE: They tried to keep me out, but I wasn't having that.
(*CLIVE shivers.*)
Po-faced secretaries sneered when I asked for Mr
Wortledge – died in 1975, apparently. So I asked for Mr
Rumble and they sneered some more and said Mr
Rumble Senior or young Mr Ben, not that either of them
would dream of seeing me without an appointment. But I
saw a door marked Mr Ben Rumble, so I whizzed in,
leaving them squawking outside. And there he was –
(*Silence.*)

CLIVE: Well? Go on –

KATE: Mm? Oh. Sorry. Yes. Well there he was with his feet on the desk having a nap. And I looked at him. And he opened his eyes. And –
(*Her voice dies away. CLIVE stands goggling with duster in his hand.*)

CLIVE: And – ? Go on. What happened?

KATE: I fell in love, of course – you stupid or something? I fell in love as he opened his eyes.

CLIVE: Oh, dear.

KATE: What do you mean 'Oh dear?' Fish got to swim, haven't they? Birds got to fly – don't you know anything? This is the first, the last, the only one. I had to learn a poem at school – in dialect, I hate dialect, and on top of that I thought it was soppy. 'And I will love thee still, my dear, till a' the seas gang dry.' Well, now it makes sense and the dialect doesn't even matter. Because I'm going to love Ben that long. Till a' the seas gang dry.

CLIVE: (*Apprehensive.*) Oh, do be careful – don't rush in – make sure he feels the same –

KATE: He does.

CLIVE: Then that's splendid, Kate. Wonderful.

KATE: *No.* It's just begun well. Give it a month and I'll scare him off – it'll be like always. Because I never see trouble coming and I don't know what I'm doing. Everyone else knows what they're up to – Aunt Deborah has all that dust to destroy and Uncle Giles has those horrid busts to polish – and you, look at you – get up, feed the goldfish – hi there, Percy, another wet day. Everyone in the whole world knows what they're doing except me. So I'll mess things up just like always only this time it'll be worse – much worse. Because he's the one – oh, is he ever the one. And if he goes – well, I won't die, of course not. But it'll be all up with me.
(*She sits, looks at CLIVE.*)
I see now why I go wrong. Most people have an upbringing – I didn't. There was no one to teach me how to behave. Aunt Deborah taught me how to keep up

appearances, she was rabid for appearances – oh, and how to get rid of coffee stains on linen, I'm a dab hand at coffee stains. But she never taught me how to navigate – steer through the icebergs. And sooner or later you're going to meet icebergs, that's for sure, and if you can't navigate they'll scupper you.

(*She pauses, frowns. Speaks dispassionately, no trace of self-pity.*)

And of course no one ever loved me. It must help if someone loves you. Quite a lot, I should think. You'd feel so confident. So most of what's wrong with me is due to lack of love, I know that, well a fat lot of good knowing does – changes nothing. And it's too late to have an upbringing. But – listen, Clive.

(*She gets up, stands by table.*)

I've had an idea – something that would – well, patch me up. (*Pause.*) I'd stop frightening people if I had a friend. Someone sensible to say slow down, Kate – hold back. If I had a friend, a permanent sure friend, the job – the lover – would get less of me. I'd be quieter –

(*Pause. CLIVE is polishing, frowning.*)

Clive. If I had a friend I'd come out mild. (*Pause.*) And if I came out mild Ben and I would be together till a' the seas gang dry. (*Pause.*) So will you be it? Will you be my friend?

(*Pause. He puts down duster and stands thinking. She watches him anxiously.*)

CLIVE: I'm sorry – I can't. Things don't happen like that.

KATE: Why not? (*Shouts.*) I like you.

CLIVE: Friends have something in common. My Aunt and Lumpkin, they're friends. They've been bumming about on racecourses shouting at each other and having a nice time for years – they're cemented. But it happened by accident – they had a shared interest and it grew. Asking someone to be your friend is meaningless. I'm sorry. I'm really sorry.

KATE: But you're not listening – you don't understand. How often does anyone have a chance to help someone else? Really help them? Well, you have, now. If you were my friend I could navigate – steer straight through the icebergs and into clear water. With Ben. (*Shouts.*) Help! Get me through the icebergs.

CLIVE: No, Kate, no. I can't do it. How can I say I'm your friend just because you think having a friend would sort you out? It would be false.

(*Silence.*)

KATE: Goodbye Ben.

CLIVE: Oh, come on, you're a big strong girl. You can manage –

KATE: No. I can't. Because I don't know why I scare people off. And if I don't know now I never will.

(*CLIVE opens his mouth to answer, but she goes on, frowning.*)

Perhaps it's something quite small. Something I just haven't thought of. Aunt Deborah used to say my feet were too big. Most days she said it. Well, perhaps that's it. Perhaps my feet alarm people. All right – they're big. And why not? Got work to do, haven't they? Race to the shops, run for a bus – six months and you're halfway to Budapest – live to be seventy and you've walked twice round the world – (*Shouts, fury.*) you need big feet, everyone should have 'em –

CLIVE: Kate.

(*She looks at him. Silence.*)

Why don't you just cry?

(*She dissolves, runs to the door. Gasps. GWYNNE comes in fast, quiet.*)

GWYNNE: Another lovely day. Always meet when the weather's fine, don't we? On your way, were you, Miss Hammond?

(*He holds the door, she goes, he shuts door. CLIVE opens his mouth.*)

How did we know you were here? This flat is watched all the time. When you come calling I am told. At once.

(*He looks at open letters, shakes his head.*)
Don't you think we would have intercepted anything of
interest? Really, Mr Warren. (*Pause.*) Sit down.
(*CLIVE sits. GWYNNE sits at table, facing him; looks at
him long.*)
I am getting nowhere. So I'm going to confide in you –
to gain your co-operation, you understand.
(*Picks up marrow scoop, glares at it.*)
Last week, seeing the stress this case was causing me,
Mrs Gwynne cooked my favourite dish. Boned leg of
lamb, stuffed with kidneys and herbs, scented with
rosemary and thyme. A rare treat.
(*He puts down marrow scoop.*)
I toyed with a mouthful and pushed the plate away. I
could not eat it. I could not eat Mrs Gwynne's roast
lamb. Imagine her astonishment. Her dismay.
(*He leans forward.*)
And why could I not eat it? Because of you. You have
played havoc with my peace of mind, and now – now
you have disrupted the serenity of my domestic life. And
all because I cannot prove your guilt.
(*He sits back, glares at CLIVE.*)
And because I cannot prove it, an element of doubt
tortures me. Are you guilty? I feel sure of it, and yet –
(*He gets up.*)
For my very sanity, I must know the answer. So we will
stay in this room until I have found your marrow, your
essence. I am going to delve into your past – back to the
womb, if need be. I want the truth. Must have it. Will
have it. Give it to me.
(*CLIVE sighs. GWYNNE settles down, lines up pen, paper.*)
Were you bright at school?
CLIVE: Yes – no – normal.
GWYNNE: Normal, that's nice –
(*He makes a note.*)
You know how to swim?
CLIVE: Yes.

GWYNNE: You swim with the tide?

CLIVE: What – ? I'm sorry. I don't understand.

GWYNNE: You're left-handed. How does it affect you?

CLIVE: Not at all.

GWYNNE: Do you excel at anything?

CLIVE: No – oh, well, mathematics, of course –

GWYNNE: So. You can add.

(*Makes a note, passes CLIVE pen and paper.*)

17 times 62.

(*CLIVE ignores paper, answers immediately.*)

CLIVE: 1054.

GWYNNE: Murder is serious. Answer.

CLIVE: (*Surprised.*) I have.

(*GWYNNE takes out calculator. Checks.*)

A calculator? For a simple sum like that? Really.

GWYNNE: 1054. (*Frowns.*) 92 x 72 x 83 –

(*He starts working on calculator; CLIVE answers at once.*)

CLIVE: 549,792.

(*GWYNNE looks at calculator, at CLIVE. Goggles.*)

It's only adding. In Sleeman's Bank any office boy can add.

GWYNNE: Sleeman's Bank? What do you know of Sleeman's Bank?

CLIVE: I worked there for twenty years.

GWYNNE: You told me you worked in a bookshop. A quiet backwater specialising in mild, harmless nonsense – the beauty of the English countryside, do-it-yourself yoga, flower arrangement. Now you tell me you belong to the real world. The best mathematical brains in the business work at Sleeman's.

CLIVE: Well? All my family's good at something – with me it's maths. Oh – and housework. Yes, I'm good at housework. Most people aren't – never bother to dust under –

GWYNNE: (*Interrupting.*) Why did you leave Sleeman's?

CLIVE: It changed. The people changed.

GWYNNE: Be specific.

CLIVE: They took my fire away.

(*Pause. GWYNNE watches him motionless, pen in hand.*)
Mr Baxendall gave it to me when he retired – he'd had it
for thirty years. One of the elements had broken in 1992,
but it was kind of Mr Baxendall to give it to me.
Sleeman's was a happy place then – people respected
each other and each other's work. But it got taken over
by managers, accountants, administrators. They had no
respect for anything but money – oh, and image. Image
was life to them – they had speech therapy to change
their vowels. Mr Baxendall would have had something to
say to them, my word yes. But Mr Baxendall knew what
was what, and they didn't.

(*GWYNNE sits motionless, his pen a little lower; CLIVE
broods.*)
One of the new lot – a horrid man, arrogant and
obsequious, with a neighing laugh somewhere between a
sheep's bray and a vomit – went sneaking to the office
managers about how inappropriate my fire was to the
firm's new image. And my fire just disappeared. He
came and told me what he'd done – he was proud of it.

(*Silence. He broods. GWYNNE sits motionless.*)
And I thought about that nice, human Mr Baxendall, and
I suppose I saw red, because I found I was beating the
little turd's head against the floor – they had to pull me
off him. Well, (*Laughs reminiscently.*) I suppose I might
have killed him. He made an awful fuss. Didn't get much
sympathy, no one liked him. They wanted me to stay on
– no one else could cope with the Central European
currencies. But I resigned. Couldn't stand the place one
more day.

(*He looks at GWYNNE.*)
I must say, you're a very good listener – sympathetic. I
expect everyone tells you things.

(*GWYNNE is absolutely motionless. Silence. Very slowly,
tidily, he puts down his pen, gazes at the ceiling.*)

GWYNNE: Oh, Mrs Gwynne, Mrs Gwynne, you are the
serpent of old Nile, Mrs Gwynne –
(*Sits forward, smiles wolfishly at CLIVE.*)
On difficult cases, I consult my wife – usually in the
garden at dusk, when she is dealing death. She likes a
crusade on hand – red spider, slugs, snails – a great one
for the holy wars is Mrs G. While she has the spray in
her hand and is cutting a swathe of death through the
insect world, her mind is abstracted but her perceptions
heightened, so last night, finding her at her ease creating
mayhem among the roses, I asked her opinion. Of you.
'His apparent mildness has confused you, Owen,' she
said. 'It is only skin deep. He is a killer.'
(*He sits back.*)
She sussed you from the start, did Mrs G. And she was
right, the stumbling block was your apparent mildness. It
confused me. But now the demon of introspection has
left me, I have no doubts.

CLIVE: I did not kill my Aunt.

GWYNNE: Oh, but you did. Now truth is out, and I have it
by the jugular. I have never been so sure of anyone's
guilt. I will tell you just how certain I am. Mrs G has
been urging me to leave the force and join her in setting
up a market garden. And if I turn out to be wrong about
you my confidence in my judgement will be shattered –
I will tear up my card, eat it, and join Mrs G in the
smiling Shropshire vales.
(*Moves half out of his chair, confronts CLIVE.*)
But I am not wrong. You killed the old lady in one of
your violent fits, your angry moods. Your lunatic temper
surprised you, and you destroyed an innocent life.
(*He gets up.*)
You are coming to the station where you will be charged
with the murder of Professor Dorothea Delaney, time
and place of deed so far unknown.

CLIVE: But there's no body –

GWYNNE: – as yet. But once you are comfortably in your cell, and have had time to consider, you will lead us to it. You will do that for us, Mr Warren. Won't you?

Scene Five

Two weeks later. AUNT's flat, empty. Sound of fumbling at the door, and AUNT comes in, a very frightened old woman. She is carrying case and bag. Drops them, stands leaning against the door, peering round, wary. Picks up bag, slowly, puts it on the table. Stands. Jumps at a noise.

AUNT: Jack. Help –
(*Takes Darwin out of bag.*)
Dolly. This won't do. Take a grip.
(*She opens Darwin, turns pages. Stops. Reads a passage, voice beginning weak, but getting stronger.*)
'When I view all beings not as special creations, but as the lineal descendants of some few beings which lived long before the first bed of the Silurian system was deposited, they seem to me to become ennobled.'
(*Shuts book.*)
That means you, Dolly. And as an ennobled being you have no right to be afraid of anything on earth. So pull yourself together.
(*She finds space on bookshelf, shoves book in.*)
Darwin will see you through. Running away, indeed. He'd have no time for that. Face the music and dance and blow all to buggery, that's what Darwin would have said.
(*She sings, cracked voice.*)
'There may be trouble ahead –' (*Stops.*) Bound to be, there always is. Keep going, Dolly. Sing along o' Darwin and don't lose your –
(*Doorbell goes. She stands petrified. Pulls herself together, goes to door, desperate.*)
– nerve.

(*Flings door open. KATE comes in. They stand. Look at each other. Silence.*)

KATE: I'm Kate.

AUNT: No need to tell me. I'd know that voice anywhere.

KATE: So you're the monster who reduced Dawn to a jelly.

(*Gratified smirk from AUNT. KATE clocks it, glares. AUNT switches it off.*)

(*Fury.*) But that's nothing to the way you treat Clive – how could you be so ungrateful to such a kind man? He does everything for you and you don't even notice. He spends hours polishing your table and you slosh whisky all over it, burn it with cigarette ends – shame on you –

AUNT: (*Puzzled.*) Polishes it, does he? Why?

KATE: – telling him he couldn't join the vagabonds – you meant to wound and you did. Good at wounding, aren't you? Oh, you've a lot to answer for. Gobi Desert, indeed, what would poor Clive do in the Gobi Desert?

AUNT: Very little, I suppose.

(*She considers.*)

Apart from sharing the black tents of the Uzbecks, stalking the great horned *ovis poli* over the fastnesses of the Altai Shan, racing snarling red camels on the old silk route to Samarkand, feasting in the green oases of Kashgar and Yarkand and riding hell for leather for Bukhara, absolutely nothing. (*Pause.*) Be bored stiff.

(*She rounds on KATE.*)

He'd escape from the stultifying life he leads in that dreary suburb.

KATE: He's perfectly happy in south Kensington.

AUNT: Why? We've only got one life and he sits playing dominoes with Percy – how dare he?

KATE: All right, he's a wimp. But he's a wimp with backbone – sticks up for anything he thinks is right and couldn't tell a lie to save his life. He's kind and he's loyal, especially to you. And all you do in return is make him doubt himself. I'm sorry, but I think you're horrible.

(*Silence. AUNT looks at her.*)

AUNT: Have a drink.

(*KATE glares, helps herself.*)

I like you. Like the way you stick up for Clive. How did you know I was here?

KATE: Hunter's instinct. You're always in my mind. Today I knew you were back. You've been with Mr Lumpkin, of course, having the time of your life. Racing, shouting –

AUNT: It was wonderful. I found my place in the world – hoped to die in it –

KATE: Why come back? And don't say conscience, you haven't bumped into yours for years.

AUNT: I got pneumonia. More or less unconscious for weeks. Lumpkin said he couldn't leave me to die on my own, sat by my bed glaring. His sick-bed manner is appalling. Then I found he'd missed Newbury to stay with me. Well, I can't have anyone upsetting their life on my account. So when I got better I ran away. Now I've stopped running. It doesn't work. But what to do next I don't know.

KATE: You could start by getting Clive out of jail.

AUNT: Jail? Clive? What – ? What's the charge?

KATE: Murder.

(*AUNT slams down her glass. Gobbles.*)

AUNT: Oh, don't be absurd. Who do they think he murdered?

KATE: You.

AUNT: Don't be ridiculous. I'm here.

KATE: Tell that to Sergeant Gwynne.

(*AUNT heads for telephone, urgent.*)

AUNT: Quick! What's his number?

KATE: Don't bother. The flat's watched, he'll have known the moment you came through the door. Surprised he's not here already.

AUNT: Why wasn't I told?

KATE: You were off with the vagabonds, remember? Over the hills and a long way off, footloose and fancy-free,

leaving poor Clive incarcerated and questioned every
day about where he hid the body – thank you, Auntie,
what a kind Auntie – even Aunt Deborah never sunk so
low.

(*Doorbell. AUNT rushes to open it. LUMPKIN storms in,
furious.*)

AUNT: Lumpkin! What are you doing here?

LUMPKIN: Sneaking off without a by-your-leave, what are
you playing at?

AUNT: You missed Newbury because of me and I won't
have it.

LUMPKIN: Newbury? Bugger Newbury – today's Gold
Cup Day and I'm not there –

AUNT: (*Horror.*) Today? It can't be – oh, I don't know one
day from another since that damn pneumonia.

LUMPKIN: First time I've missed it since I was three years
old sitting high on my brother's shoulders.

AUNT: Then what the hell are you doing here?

LUMPKIN: I had to see you were all right. You're Jack's
widow. I'm responsible.

(*AUNT sits with a thump, shocked and furious. LUMPKIN
pours himself whisky.*)

I'm responsible whether you – or I – like it or not. I'm
the one who'll be around to close your eyes. Now Jack's
gone no one else has the right. Grow up, Duchess.

(*She opens her mouth.*)

And shut up. I haven't finished. It was irresponsible
running away. And cowardly. Couldn't face me to say
what you were doing. Now that's not your character and
I don't like it. Friends should stay as you chose 'em and
not go around being different. I'm used to you the way
you are.

AUNT: Sorry, Lumpkin. I've given you a lot of trouble.

LUMPKIN: (*Fury.*) Listen to yourself. You've never given a
tinker's curse how much trouble you gave. Be yourself,
give trouble, that's all I ask. Suppose one day I opened
Treasure Island and found Blind Pew king of the castle on

the last page instead of dying the horrible death in Chapter Five which is his wont, how would I feel I ask you? Luckily Pew knows what's expected of him and dies in the same place every time. Be like Pew. Know your place and stick in it.

AUNT: I'm sorry.

LUMPKIN: (*Explodes.*) For Christ's sake – there you go again. Friends don't apologise, they spit in your eye.

AUNT: Lumpkin – did you put the money on?

(*Silence. LUMPKIN takes out cigar, lights it.*)

LUMPKIN: No.

(*She opens her mouth.*)

I won't do it. Won't. Won't. Won't. You made me your bank. Banks are responsible, or they used to be. I'm an old-fashioned bank, and I will not put money you entrusted me with on a horse that runs oblivious of the winning post. He doesn't avoid it, just hasn't noticed it. I don't know what he's dreaming of – dining on oats with caviare, starring as guest horse on *Coronation Street* – but the idea of winning hasn't entered his half-baked mind.

AUNT: It's the only way to fund Jack's chair. I can't die till it's settled.

LUMPKIN: You'll go when you're called for.

AUNT: Not till I've funded his chair I won't.

(*Pause. LUMPKIN smashes his glass down.*)

LUMPKIN: Bloody doctors – they told me to keep it from you for your own good – they were wrong. You've a right to know. (*Pause.*) You've three months to live and that's if you're lucky. So it's no time to be fussing about Jack's chair. It's over.

(*He slumps in chair. Silence.*)

AUNT: Dying, eh?

(*She frowns. Silence. Then she speaks quietly, conversationally.*)

Lumpkin. I don't think you've really examined Clouds of Glory's breeding. You haven't looked back to Swynford.

LUMPKIN: Oh, Lumpkin, what a slapdash fellow you are. How could you overlook a horse foaled in 1905? How –?

AUNT: 1907. Your ignorance is appalling. Swynford won the St Leger, the Eclipse Stakes, the Hardwicke Stakes – twice – the Coronation Cup. He's the male ancestor of Bahram, Big Game, Blenheim, Alcydon – and Clouds of Glory. Clouds of Glory has Swynford's blood twenty times over – Swynford who was by John of Gaunt, who was by Isinglass out of La Fleche – oh, what a great mare, what a non-pareil – full sister to St Simon out of Quiver – it's a double treble dose of the Eclipse line at its very best.

(Pause. She shouts.)

And now, you old fool, put that money on. This is my death wish. My last bet.

(She gets up, stands over him.)

Well? Want me to curse you from beyond the grave?

(LUMPKIN shudders.)

Better get on with it then, hadn't you? Now.

(Long silence. Then LUMPKIN gets out his mobile.)

LUMPKIN: I'll take it next door. Don't want you breathing down my neck.

(He lumbers off with his mobile. AUNT breathes a sigh of relief.)

AUNT: Whew. Never thought the old fool would see sense –

KATE: I'm sorry about – about –

AUNT: Don't be. If I can fund Jack's chair I'll be ready to die. I think. Well. *(Pause.)* When I was a child in Somerset my governess used to drive me in a donkey cart to the main road to see the cars go by. For a treat. Sometimes there were no cars all day – not one. Now there are bits of space capsule flying around in the atmosphere, may bump into us at any moment – what an invigorating world. Perhaps I'll never be ready to go –

(Doorbell rings. KATE answers it. CLIVE and GWYNNE come in.)

(*To CLIVE.*) Ah! Seen sense have they? Damn fools, locking you up. Murderer? Why, you couldn't kill a slug in a lettuce.

(*GWYNNE looks at AUNT, goes over to bookcase, takes out book, looks at picture on back cover.*)

CLIVE: Well? Go on, arrest her.

KATE: What for?

CLIVE: Singing 'Dear Little Buttercup' off-key, drinking whisky for elevenses, crimes against humanity – oh, take your pick.

(*GWYNNE is looking at picture, at AUNT.*)

GWYNNE: A speaking likeness. You are Professor Delaney, no mistake. You are no dear old lady the worms have eaten, victim of a scheming nephew. You are an exuberant old party who has been cavorting on every seedy racecourse in the land. Dear old lady, heaven preserve me from such. For months I have harried an innocent man – and where was my boasted judgement then?

(*LUMPKIN comes back.*)

AUNT: What odds did you get?

LUMPKIN: 13 – 1, other punters having sense. What a fool I felt, putting all that on such a horse. Worse than foolish – ashamed.

(*He puts cigar down. AUNT takes it, absent-minded, sits at table, picks up pen, starts doing calculation.*)

GWYNNE: Well, well. Mr Tony Goldsmith, only surviving partner of the Goldsmith family firm. Why, I do believe you are the friendly bookie who takes old women's cheques for £40,000 – masquerading as Lumpkin.

LUMPKIN: I never masqueraded in my life. It was her Jack called me that – first time I met him. Chepstow March meeting – bit of spring in the air and –

AUNT / LUMPKIN: – a blue dusk.

(*LUMPKIN looks at her.*)

AUNT: There always is spring in the air and a blue dusk when you tell this story. Do shut up and let me do my sums.

LUMPKIN: (*Ignoring her.*) He said I was masquerading. I'm putting him right. There was her Jack swaying on his feet and singing 'Pretty Molly Branagan'. And I pulled him back just as he was falling under Solly Myer's Rolls. 'Who the hell are you,' he said, 'to take a gentleman by the scruff of his neck and mess up his linen?' 'Tony Goldsmith,' I said. 'Lumpkin,' he said, and he laughed. I've never heard another laugh like his. I took him on for life. On sight. I loved that man. 'Lumpkin,' he said. Never did know what he meant.

(*Glares at GWYNNE.*)

Masquerading, indeed.

(*AUNT throws down pen.*)

AUNT: 13–1. That'll do it. Home and dried.

(*She beams at CLIVE, who is sitting slumped and gloomy. He doesn't respond. GWYNNE gets up.*)

GWYNNE: I will go next door and compose a statement for your bank. You shall sign it. It will set their minds at rest if you skedaddle to Doncaster. For a lark.

(*He goes. LUMPKIN clocks his cigar, bemused. AUNT hands it back. CLIVE sits slumped, KATE glares at him.*)

KATE: You might at least look pleased to see her.

CLIVE: (*Savage.*) Why? I've had 14 days in jail, no books in my cell, nothing to do but think about what you said when I was polishing the table and trying not to hear. (*To AUNT.*) Kate said you only bothered about me when there was no one better around. I'd always known, really. Just didn't admit it. Until Uncle Jack died you didn't give me the time of day.

KATE: I should never have said it.

CLIVE: Why not, it's true. Until Uncle Jack died you never got in touch – didn't lift a telephone. And I tried, over the years, remember? But you were always too busy – both of you.

(*AUNT is sitting looking old and grim.*)
It's not as though I wanted to come first, or second, or tenth, come to that. I just wanted a place, a small but definite place. You were the only relation I had left and I think families matter. But until Uncle Jack died you had no time for me. None. And why didn't you let me know you were all right? Just a line would have done. But you didn't bother.

LUMPKIN: You should be ashamed, old girl. You're a disgrace. Just up from pneumonia and you bugger off into the blue – land your nephew in jail –

CLIVE: – worry poor Mr Lumpkin out of his mind –

LUMPKIN: I never thought I'd say this. But if I can't look after you, and your nephew can't either, I'm sorry, Duchess. But you really should be in a home.

(*AUNT looks wildly at him; leaps up, backs away.*)

AUNT: (*Screams.*) No –

(*Silence. She stands there shaking. They look at her in consternation. She sits.*)

They cornered my friend Maggie.

(*She shivers, takes a deep breath.*)

They hunted her down and locked her up. And humiliated her – oh, not intentionally, they were just stupid – so stupid. (*Shudders.*) They made her wear blue bows in her hair – I said 'Take them off.' She said 'They'll only put them on again and say "Who's a silly girl, then, don't you want to look smart?".' They forced her to watch television oh, morning, noon and night. The sun came up and the sun went down and still it droned on, on and on. Then one day they brought her Barbara Cartland when she'd asked for Maeterlinck's *Life of the Bee*, and she lost her temper, well, who wouldn't? But they decided she was giving trouble. They don't like trouble, those hounds of hell. So they gave her some filth to keep her quiet. It took her mind away. She was a cabbage in weeks.

(*She jumps up.*)

Don't let them take my mind away – please – don't let
them –
(*She stands shaking. Silence.*)
LUMPKIN: All right, old girl, all right. But blowed if I
know what we're to do with you.
(*Sighs, looks at his watch.*)
If you want to watch your money go down the drain
you'd better put the telly on.
(*AUNT looks at her watch, galvanised.*)
AUNT: Clive – the telly – quick – (*Yells.*) Move –
He puts it on, they all watch. Silence. Then telly warms up.)
NEWSREADER: (*Voice.*) In Leicestershire animal activists
have poisoned a pack of hounds because of their cruelty
to foxes. They –
AUNT: Not that channel, you fool –
CLIVE: (*Snarls.*) Back on form, are we?
(*He gets the right channel.*)
COMMENTATOR: (*Voice.*) – into the last half mile – and
the only interest is in the placing – Roman Candle's
been forging ahead since they left the stalls – so far in
front he might be in another race. Pity there's no
challenge –
LUMPKIN: There. What did I tell you?
AUNT: Wait.
COMMENTATOR: (*Voice.*) He's a good ten lengths ahead –
just cruising –
LUMPKIN: If Jack was here he'd kill me –
AUNT: Wait.
COMMENTATOR: (*Voice.*) Shame there's no opposition –
LUMPKIN: Oh, switch off, I can't bear to watch –
AUNT: Wait.
COMMENTATOR: (*Voice.*) Well, there he goes. Let's have a
look at the rest of the field, let's – (*Stops.*) Hang on –
what's – good heavens, what a magnificent – well, I said
Roman Candle needed opposition, if only this horse had
started his run earlier we'd have had a great race –
Clouds of Glory, a total outsider – well, we'll certainly

be watching him next time out – it's extraordinary – I've
never seen such a run – it's not possible – he's going like
– well, in all my days –
(*LUMPKIN is gobbling, AUNT calm. The crowd is gasping,
then roaring.*)
(*Screech.*) He's coming – he's going to win – Clouds of
Glory's going to win –
(*Crowd roars, then goes totally silent. Groans.*)
No. Roman Candle just held him off – one more stride
and he'd have done it. What an extr –
(*LUMPKIN switches telly off. AUNT sits motionless.*)
LUMPKIN: Well. He gave you a run.
(*Silence. They look at her. KATE dives in her bag, produces
letter, waves it under AUNT's nose. She brushes it aside,
starts twisting her hands together.*)
AUNT: (*To herself.*) I've lost Jack's chair – oh, what am I to
do?
LUMPKIN: (*Fury.*) Look – I told you – you're dying.
What's the point in fussing over a chair?
AUNT: (*Desperate.*) Stop saying I'm dying. I can't. Not yet –
LUMPKIN: You've no choice. Accept it. And go out like
you've lived – don't diminish yourself. You've always
had sense. And dignity. Don't lose them now at the end.
AUNT: I can't die owing Jack –
LUMPKIN: Forty good years you had together – isn't that
enough?
AUNT: I never gave him children.
(*She drains her glass.*)
They would have been his memorial. We both wanted
them. But we kept saying next month, next year – oh,
after Ascot – you know what it's like – Cheltenham
coming up, then it's whizzed by before you notice. Like
the years. I was 38 when I married. Before I could look
round it was too late.
(*LUMPKIN refills her glass; she drinks.*)
I've had great days. The friends and the horses and the
books. Sky and space. And Jack – above all, Jack. But if

I'm to die letting him down I wish none of it had ever happened.

(*She turns to CLIVE.*)

What you said is true. When Jack was alive I didn't give a tinker's curse for anyone else. We were complete. When he died – well. I was lucky, Lumpkin was there. But this flat – I couldn't read for the silence. Then I asked you round, and there you were, chatting away. Of course you're right, I don't listen. But you make an agreeable noise, and I like it. And our outings were fun. I'm in your debt. I was foolish and arrogant telling you to do things you don't want to do. I've been a bad aunt to you.

CLIVE: You made me laugh. Gave me company when I had none. Our Saturdays were the high spot of the week. So don't talk rubbish..

AUNT: I've come to the end and got everything wrong.

LUMPKIN: Nonsense.

AUNT: Oh, shut up. Don't try to console me as though I'd played a bad hand at bridge. I'm dying and I've made a mess of everything. What consolation can there possibly be? Do show a little sense –

(*KATE shoves letter under her nose; she brushes it away.*)

What can I do? Can't any of you suggest something? Oh, you're useless –

CLIVE: In my opinion, if you ask me, you're behaving like a spoilt child. We all fail at almost everything, why should you be an exception? You wanted a chair in Uncle Jack's memory, you can't have it, so you're taking it out on us. Well, that's my opinion. If you ask me.

(*AUNT glares at him.*)

And are you going to spend your last months being disagreeable because you can't get what you want? What fond memories we'll have. Put it on your tombstone, shall we? 'She Died Snarling.' I don't think much of that.

LUMPKIN: And what would Jack say? He always accepted what was – didn't make silly scenes and upset people.

Think of the trillions of dead out there – lots of 'em must have deserved a memorial, but they didn't get it – in blessed memory on the tombstone if they were lucky, until the tombstone crumbled. Means nothing. They're forgotten and we'll be forgotten like the rest and so what?

AUNT: (*Fury.*) Don't need three months, then, do I? Might as well go to bed now and never get up.

LUMPKIN: None of that. Pull yourself together.

AUNT: All right. I accept. I've failed Jack and he'll be forgotten.

CLIVE: As we all will.

LUMPKIN: You must do better than that. Got to come through cheerful. Have a bit of respect.

AUNT: What for?

LUMPKIN: Life.

(*Silence.*)

AUNT: All right, Lumpkin.

LUMPKIN: It's still Ascot tomorrow. We'll argue over the runners – have a nice quarrel. That'll cheer you.

AUNT: All right, Lumpkin.

LUMPKIN: (*Shouts.*) For Christ's sake stop being mild. Snarl! Be yourself –

(*AUNT sits, morose. KATE holds letter under her nose. She takes it, lacklustre.*)

KATE: A publisher gave me this to give to you.

AUNT: Then why didn't you?

(*KATE opens her mouth in fury; AUNT opens letter; reads it, puzzled, then amazed.*)

Who is this man? He wants to publish my journal and give me a £50,000 advance –

(*She throws down the letter, fury.*)

And it's too late. Why didn't it happen before? I could have turned it into half a million – but time's run out –

KATE: (*Fury.*) You don't need a penny, you – you old twerp.

(*AUNT looks at her bewildered.*)

143

The diary's going to be published. That's your Jack's memorial. He'll speak for himself – his words, his jokes. And if he's what you think, people will still be laughing in fifty years – a hundred. Who wants a chair?

(*Silence. They all watch AUNT, who is sitting motionless.*)

AUNT: My word. (*Silence.*) My word. (*Silence.*) So easy – all the time. And I never saw. So easy.

(*Sudden vigour. She bustles to desk, sits, writes, fast and silent. They watch her.*)

Writing a codicil to my will.

(*She writes. Silence. Writes while she talks.*)

Says Clive is to deal with the publishing and do what he likes with the proceeds. Lumpkin – come and sign.

(*LUMPKIN signs. AUNT beckons to KATE, who comes over, signs. AUNT puts down paper, starts writing another sheet.*)

(*To CLIVE.*) Jack's journal now belongs to you.

CLIVE: (*Horrified.*) But the responsibility –

AUNT: – is yours.

(*She glares at him, goes back to writing.*)

One last debt –

(*Writes. Stops. Puts paper tidily on desk. Passes publisher's letter to CLIVE.*)

I'll need the £50,000. Get it for me, will you, Clive? Fast.

(*Gets up.*)

Three months. Might manage the autumn meeting at Cheltenham. (*Beams.*) No old folks home for me – what a time we'll have, Lumpkin. Why, it's a fairy tale – of limited duration, of course, due to mortality, but who's counting? And when I go crashing into eternity it won't matter. Either Darwin was wrong and I'll be with Jack or he's right and I'm for oblivion.

(*Looks at LUMPKIN. Cackles.*)

Odds on oblivion, eh Lumpkin?

(*GWYNNE comes back; hands AUNT piece of paper. She signs.*)

Took your time.

GWYNNE: I was composing my letter of resignation from the Force.

CLIVE: Oh, please – not because of me. It really doesn't matter –

GWYNNE: It matters. Puffed up with professional pride, I counted myself among the crack troops, knew the superb arrogance of the Praetorian Guard. (*To KATE.*) You were right. I thought I knew the human heart, but only God knows that. He is not mocked.

CLIVE: Look, I'm free. It was a small thing.

GWYNNE: Not small to me. It has destroyed what was my life, and no man's life is nothing.

CLIVE: Sergeant –

GWYNNE: Sergeant no more.
(*He goes to desk, picks up scissors, takes out his card, looks at it.*)
'Farewell the plumed troops, and the big wars –'
(*Begins to snip his card.*)
Everyone's dignity should be preserved. But I would have none if I clung to a profession where my failure has been so spectacular. My knowledge of human nature has been shown to be non-existent. So my future path will lie where such knowledge is irrelevant. I will do as Mrs G wishes, we will start a market garden. But I have had enough of villainy. The pursuit and destruction of the criminals of the garden world – the aphid, the slug – I will leave to Mrs G. My lot will be to tend and nurture the plants. My life will be spent among the scent of roses, rich, sensuous crimson, ethereal white. I will watch the dew on their petals at dawn. In the evening I will enjoy Mrs Gwynne's roast lamb. My sleep will be dreamless.
(*GWYNNE looks at fragments of card.*)
And in this quiet world, God grant I find salvation at my latter end.
(*He puts fragments in waste paper basket.*)

CLIVE: You were going to –
(*Pause. He catches GWYNNE's eye.*)

(*Quiet.*) – eat them.

(*GWYNNE gives him a look. Puts scissors back tidily.*)

GWYNNE: I have had enough of you, sir. And your dear
old Auntie. I've had enough of the pack of you. I take
my leave with no regrets.

(*Goes out, shuts door.*)

CLIVE: Well you've messed his life up all right.

AUNT: (*Beams.*) Oh, Lumpkin, I'm a happy woman. All
debts paid.

CLIVE: Well, congratulations. And what about Lumpkin?
After all these years? And what about –

AUNT: Oh, how selfish I am –

CLIVE: (*Quiet.*) – me?

AUNT: (*To LUMPKIN.*) You'll be very alone when I die. You
should make a plan – now –

LUMPKIN: Well. Tad's dead, Jack's dead. When you die,
there'll be nothing to keep me here. (*Broods.*) I might
head for Samoa.

AUNT: The South Seas? I say, Lumpkin, that's going it –

LUMPKIN: I could keep an eye on Stevenson's grave. I
owe him. That book's meant more to me –
'Under a wide and starry sky
Dig my grave and let me lie.'
That's what he wanted. Well, better have a look, hadn't I?
See there's no weeds growing between him and the
stars –

AUNT: Suppose he's set in concrete?

LUMPKIN: I'll deal with that when the time comes. Think
I'll settle out there, have a vegetable patch. Paw paws –
bananas –

AUNT: Paw – paws – my word. I can see you, Lumpkin.
Blue skies – blue seas – drink in one hand –

LUMPKIN: I'll think of Redcar in the rain. Don't think I'll
miss it.

AUNT: You'll have time to read his other books –

(*LUMPKIN looks baffled, incredulous.*)

LUMPKIN: Other – ? He wrote other books? Why didn't you tell me?

AUNT: Thought you knew.

(*LUMPKIN thinks, frowns.*)

LUMPKIN: How many? How many other books?

AUNT: Oh – twenty? (*Pause.*) You've worlds to find, Lumpkin. Worlds to find.

(*He thinks. Gives her a lovely smile.*)

LUMPKIN: Yes.

AUNT: (*Brisk.*) Well, come along, no time to waste – where's my *Origin of Species*? And *Timeform* –

(*She gets up, finds them, crashes onto sofa, passes out. They all rush to her. Silence. LUMPKIN fills her glass. She sits up slowly, drinks.*)

My word. It's coming nearer.

(*She breathes deeply, then turns to LUMPKIN, urgent.*)

Lumpkin. Don't let me have a deathbed conversion. Let me die as I lived. No truck with God. If he exists – and he wants me – he can find me.

LUMPKIN: If he exists. And he wants you. I daresay he will. (*Pause.*) Such arrogance.

AUNT: And if I don't quite die, finish me off, there's a good chap.

CLIVE: You can't ask him to kill you –

AUNT: Why not, he's my friend. (*To LUMPKIN.*) Have me cremated – scatter the ashes on the next course you come to – what are you scowling at?

LUMPKIN: Suppose it's Redcar. I hate that course. Wouldn't like to think of you blowing in the wind at Redcar.

AUNT: Well hang on to the ashes till you get to Newbury. An urn isn't much to carry – a little dust. But if you lose it on the way I won't haunt you.

(*She struggles up, picks up Darwin and* Timeform. *Pauses. Puts down Darwin.*)

I won't take Darwin. Don't think he'll help.

(*She stops. Looks puzzled.*)

147

It's not what I thought –

LUMPKIN: What isn't?

AUNT: I don't know. Anything.

(*She heads for door, brisk.*)

Come along, Lumpkin, do – bring that bag –

(*LUMPKIN picks up bag, follows her out. Her voice is heard off.*)

(*Off.*) Oysters tonight. We're celebrating. I may eat a barrelful. And have you ever had enough caviare? At one sitting? I haven't. But I'm going to. Now or never, isn't it?

(*KATE runs to the door after her, stops dead. AUNT's voice further away.*)

(*Off.*) – might toy with some devilled kidneys –

(*Voice trails off downstairs, sound of feet dies away. Silence.*)

KATE: She's gone.

(*Voice trails off downstairs, sound of feet dies away.*)

(*Fury.*) She was the one person who could have taught me to navigate, why didn't I ask her? Why? Ben and I would have sailed in clear water for the rest of our days. But she's gone, and the icebergs will scupper me – shove me under the freezing water – squat there laughing their silly heads off – oh, why didn't I ask her?

CLIVE: I wish she'd said goodbye.

KATE: Oh Clive. I'm so sorry. How selfish I am, it's far worse for you –

CLIVE: She didn't even look back. Just went.

(*Gets up, goes to table, heavy. Picks up paper, sighs.*)

This codicil will mean a lot of respon –

(*He stops. Picks up another piece of paper.*)

What's this? (*Pause.*) 'Dear Clive – in great haste – I don't think we'll meet again and I really cannot bear to say goodbye. I can never thank you enough for making so many days happy which without you would have been lonely and bleak. Don't let that damn greengrocer bully you – stick up for yourself – your devoted and attached Aunt Dolly Delaney.'

(*Silence.*)

She always knew how to win a person back.

(*He folds up letter, puts it in his pocket, carefully. KATE gets up, goes to door, turns.*)

KATE: Here – have these. I bought them for her.

(*She shoves paper bag at him; he looks at it suspiciously.*)

CLIVE: Strawberries? Strawberries are out of season.

KATE: So what? Supermarkets always have them.

(*CLIVE sniffs one; looks disgusted.*)

CLIVE: How much did you pay?

KATE: You think I'd remember? Shopping's so dull.

(*CLIVE sits heavily, stares at her.*)

CLIVE: Dull. You shop in supermarkets. You buy fruit out of season. You don't care about the price. (*Shouts – fury.*) Of course you find shopping dull.

(*Glares. She looks totally bewildered, upset.*)

I'm sorry. Without Aunt Dolly to teach me I would have been as ignorant as you. Well. Almost.

(*Silence. He frowns.*)

I suppose I'd better take you in hand – like she did me.

KATE: (*Uninterested.*) Well, I've got the odd morning free –

CLIVE: (*Shocked.*) The odd morning? You mad? Shopping is an art, think you can master an art in the odd morning? Years, it'll take years –

KATE: (*Incredulous.*) Years?

CLIVE: First you must study Muffet –

(*He starts riffling through shelves looking for book.*)

A M Muffet. *The Intelligent Shopper's Guide to Fish Fowl and Fruit.* A masterpiece. Oh, where's she put it?

(*KATE starts laughing.*)

KATE: *Years?* Why, we'll be – we'll be –

(*She stops. Frowns. CLIVE is still riffling.*)

CLIVE: Ruff's *Guide to the Turf* – Newton's *Principia* –

KATE: (*Very quiet.*) Like your Aunt –

(*Slowly light dawns. CLIVE is tossing books about, muttering.*)

– and Lumpkin. Cemented. Like your Aunt and
Lumpkin. (*Pause. Amazed.*) I've got a friend. (*She sits,
stunned.*) Icebergs? They're a busted flush.
(*Pause. She takes a deep breath.*)
Clear waters ahead.
(*CLIVE riffles more and more wildly, throwing books about,
muttering to himself, finds Muffet, passes it to her. She takes
it like it was the Holy Grail.*)

CLIVE: There. Oh, and you'll need *Larousse Gastronomique* –
(*He starts riffling through shelves again, muttering. She sits,
gazing at Muffet. Opens it.*)

KATE: 'Varieties of apples. The intelligent shopper
discriminates. Rejecting the Golden Delicious as tasteless
pap, he demands the elegant tang of a Russet, or the
crisp splendour of a Cox's Orange Pippin.'
(*She stops. Takes a deep breath.*)
A Cox's Orange Pippin.
(*Goes back to Muffet. Starts to read in earnest.*)

The End

THE GREAT AUNTS

CAST

MAJOR ROSS-MARTIN, Inniskillings, retired

MRS ROSS-MARTIN, his wife

Their daughters:
MAUD, late 40s
VIOLET, early 40s
HARRIET, mid 30s
CON, 25

HILDA, a maid

MR RUDD, a rich tradesman

TIME: October 1905
PLACE: The drawing-room of Major Ross-Martin's house in Central Wales.

ONE

The drawing-room of MAJOR ROSS-MARTIN's house in Central Wales on an October morning in 1905. On one side of the room are French windows between two further large windows. They look out onto lawns, bordered by shrubberies, behind which rather menacing hills loom up, a little too close to the house. The room is large and shabby; every chair needs re-upholstering and re-covering. The principal pieces of furniture – bureau book-case, work table, sofa table, etc – date from about 1800, but the chairs and sofas are from the 1860s – ie they are now nearly fifty years old and hopelessly unfashionable. There is a grand piano, and two small black heavy Indian tables inlaid with ivory, brought back from service in India by MAJOR ROSS-MARTIN. A large leather chair dominates one side of the fireplace; a small rocking chair is on the other. The walls are crammed with very dark oil paintings all portraying some aspect of death, destruction, or stormy weather.

On the floor a vast pile of clothes is being sorted by MAUD, late forties, the eldest of MAJOR ROSS-MARTIN's four daughters. She is very neat, dressed in different shades of grey. She has a kind, simple face, and is the only one of the sisters who does not look torn by seething discontent. Her movements are quiet and orderly, even though at the minute she is clearly upset.

Her sister HARRIET, mid-thirties, is standing by the French windows. Recently widowed, she is dressed in black. All the sisters are tall, but HARRIET is the tallest. She is passionate, noisy, arrogant, quick-tempered and completely self-centred. She has considerable beauty of a rather powerful kind, and grace of movement in spite of her height. Her usual expression is a furious glare; when she smiles her smile is charming. Like all the sisters except MAUD, she has vast energy and nothing to use it on.

The weather is foul. HARRIET is putting a lot of wordless passion into glaring out at the rain. MAUD is rummaging through the pile, keeps picking things up then dropping them back in disgust.

HARRIET: The rain's forgotten how to stop.

MAUD: Shameful – it's shameful –

HARRIET: We should build an ark. Before it's too late.

MAUD: Look at this –

(*She holds up decrepit-looking garment; HARRIET is still gazing out of window.*)

HARRIET: But we won't have Violet in our ark. Let her drown.

(*Speaks in exasperated fury.*)

There! Look at Hilary, out in the rain without a coat – really, Jenny must be the worst nursery maid in Wales –

(*She opens window; shouts.*)

Hilary! Go and tell Jenny to put your coat on – now! At once!

(*HARRIET closes window, stands watching.*)

She's flat-footed, you know. From Toby's side of the family, of course.

(*Admires her feet.*)

Imagine! Me with a flat-footed daughter –

(*MAUD is still holding up garment for HARRIET to look at.*)

MAUD: Harriet! I'm talking to you. Is this really the best we can do?

(*HARRIET turns with a start and comes over to pile of things.*)

HARRIET: What do you mean? I've given two petticoats, didn't you notice?

(*She riffles through pile, holds up a petticoat triumphantly.*)

There – look – where's the other one, someone's taken – oh. Here it is.

(*She examines them both.*)

MAUD: I'm ashamed of us. When I think of the lumber in this house – the clothes, the little boxes, bits of jewellery, knick-knacks, vases, belts, buckles – kickshaws –

(*HARRIET is still examining petticoats; puts them back in the pile reluctantly.*)

HARRIET: It was a sacrifice. The rest of you have only yourselves to think of, but a widow with three children has responsibilities. Those petticoats could be made into underclothes for Barbara and Hilary if Jenny wasn't so useless with her needle. Wretched girl, she would happen to me, just my luck –

MAUD: – and all we can give to the church bazaar is this pile of rubbish.

HARRIET: Rubbish?
(*She snatches up petticoat.*)
Look – years of wear –
(*Examines it closely.*)
I shall keep it.

MAUD: Oh? And what will you give in its place?

HARRIET: I shall leave the other one. That's more than enough.

MAUD: Then I must give something to make up for our meanness – my amethyst brooch, perhaps –

HARRIET: Maud! Your brooch is worth a lot of money – Grandma meant you to wear it for your lifetime then hand it down. Give it away, indeed, she'd be horrified – it's not yours to give. It belongs to Barbara or Hilary.

MAUD: Why?

HARRIET: Because neither you or Violet or Con are married, of course.

MAUD: So?

HARRIET: Don't be silly. My children are your natural heirs – your heirs, Maud, really, how slow you are. And the brooch must go to Barbara. Hilary's complexion is too sallow, it wouldn't suit her. The emeralds would, though. I must speak to Con –

MAUD: (*Shock.*) You can't ask Con to leave Hilary her emeralds –

HARRIET: Of course I won't. I'll tell her.
(*MAUD sits back on her heels and gasps.*)

What's the matter? Obviously Con will leave them to one of the children, and she might pick the wrong one. She's not very observant.

MAUD: They're her emeralds. If she throws them in the weir it's no one's business but hers.

HARRIET: Really, Maud – you're very odd sometimes. I suppose it's being a saint. I hope you don't turn into a strange old woman and embarrass us all.

MAUD: And although it's true Violet and I will never marry, Con might. Quite easily.

HARRIET: Oh, Con might marry. I suppose. If we didn't live at the back of beyond, if anyone ever came to the house and saw her – if we ever went anywhere or met anyone – yes. Con might marry.

MAUD: Anyhow it's my brooch. I shall do as I please.

HARRIET: Oh, keep the wretched petticoat –
(*She hurls it down.*)

MAUD: (*Ironic.*) Such generosity.

HARRIET: Maud – don't talk in that horrid tone. You sound like Violet –

MAUD: Or perhaps even you.

HARRIET: Me? I don't sound like that. Surely not. (*Panic.*) Do I?

MAUD: Yes. Sometimes.

HARRIET: (*Passion.*) Then why don't you stop me? Please stop me – I don't want to end up horrid like Violet –
(*Hugs MAUD.*)
And don't you start being like the rest of us – don't. You're the one person we can all trust to be good, and kind, and think the best of everyone. I may not be very nice, but I'd be much nastier if it wasn't for you, and if you turn disagreeable the world will crumble – you're our good angel –
(*She picks up petticoat again, examines it, puts it down reluctantly.*)
We can't afford to give things away. Everyone in the neighbourhood knows we can't pay our bills –

(*MAUD holds up pair of old gloves with holes in them.*)

MAUD: Violet's contribution.

(*Throws them down, riffles through jumble. Speaks with fury.*)
Oh, not her moth-eaten purse again – I told her last year it wasn't good enough.

(*Glares at HARRIET.*)
Surely Harriet, it makes you ashamed? When we have so much?

HARRIET: So much! You're joking. Cooped up here, the four of us – and one of them Violet, ugh – with Mama, who has – well, left us, I suppose you could say, and Papa, oh dear Lord, Papa –

MAUD: Look what we've given. For a roof over our heads, a moth-eaten purse. For a lifetime of ease, two old petticoats. For food every day, a broken trumpet. Is this all the thanks we can give to God? This is not giving – giving means sacrifice. We're fed and dry and warm. Think of those who aren't.

(*VIOLET comes in while she is speaking, carrying a book. There is an immediate chill in the air. In her early forties, with a supercilious, bad-tempered face and eyebrows which seem permanently raised; a lonely, isolated figure. She dresses rather defiantly; always with one fierce bit of colour somewhere – violent mauve, or saffron. She takes no notice of the others, makes for easy chair, raises her eyebrows at pile in passing. Settles down, opens her book.*)

HARRIET: Warm? In this house? What a quaint sense of humour you have. There isn't a room where the damp doesn't reach for your bones. It was never like this at Beaupré –

(*VIOLET speaks without taking her eyes from her book.*)

VIOLET: We all know, Harriet, that Beaupré was warmer, grander, and in every way superior to any house the rest of us have ever known. The elegance of the drawing room, the fine proportions of the breakfast room, are thrown in our teeth too frequently and too loudly for us to forget. Since your return not a day has gone by

without you reminding us of your former grandeur –
frequently several times.

HARRIET: Did I ask to be a penniless widow? There I was,
a married woman with a place in the world. I mattered.
And look at me now – dwindled back into being a sister.
When I married I thought I'd left here for ever – how
relieved I felt –

VIOLET: We all breathed a sigh of relief when you married.
Unfortunately it was premature.

(*As HARRIET and VIOLET snarl at each other, MAUD
looks increasingly distressed.*)

HARRIET: Oh, keep your nasty cold whipping tongue to
yourself, Violet. You're as foul as the weather.

(*She turns and glares out at the garden, shivers.*)

I looked out of this window on my wedding morning
and danced. Because I was escaping from those hills.
And here I am, twelve years older, and they're still
squatting over me. In a hundred years' time – in a
thousand – they'll still be there. And where will I be?
Please God I shan't walk this house a discontented
ghost – not an eternity of this house, oh, God, let me
sink into dust –

VIOLET: Silent dust. If you have any consideration for the
rest of us.

MAUD: Oh, stop it, stop it! What is the point?

HARRIET: There. You've upset Maud. How selfish you are,
Violet – you're not fit to live with – and stop wriggling
your nasty sandy eyebrows at me –

MAUD: Harriet!

HARRIET: Why, Maud, whatever is the matter?

MAUD: Why can't we be nicer to each other? Some
families are. Look at the Granvilles, they're so fond of
each other, they're a pleasure to be with.

HARRIET: No pleasure to us since we're forbidden to see
them. And Papa won't relent. Once he's quarrelled with
someone, that's it. What did Colonel Granville do to
upset him so much?

MAUD: I'm sure he did nothing. Quarrels always stem from Papa, you know that. But how I miss them – their hearts rise so lightly – they make each other's happiness. If we stopped tearing each other apart we might be happy like them.

HARRIET: Just what I was trying to tell Violet. I told her to keep her nasty tongue to herself. Didn't you hear?

(*MAUD sighs in exasperation.*)

MAUD: People should be happy together if they can. Think of the Mansels' picnic last summer – such fun it must have been, sixty-four of them, all cousins, on the sands at Borth –

VIOLET: What a pity there wasn't a tidal wave.

(*HARRIET laughs heartily.*)

MAUD: There! You do have something in common. You laugh at Violet's jokes.

HARRIET: Well it was funny.

MAUD: Although it wasn't a very nice thing to say, Violet dear –

(*HARRIET and VIOLET shoot a conspiratorial look at each other; but it is brief.*)

Do you remember our great picnic on those sands? Before you were married, Harriet. We had a lovely time – all four of us together. We have – sometimes – had splendid, happy days –

(*VIOLET stiffens suddenly; the other two don't notice.*)

HARRIET: That's true – it was fun –

MAUD: We laughed all the day long –

(*VIOLET rises swiftly to her feet and rushes out of the room, clearly in a passion of some sort. MAUD looks in horror.*)

Oh, how could I be so tactless –

(*HARRIET looks surprised.*)

It was the day she had the letter from Aunt Emma Holroyd saying she was off to make her will – oh, poor Violet, she was to inherit everything, including Glynn Abbot – the finest house on Anglesea –

(*HARRIET snorts.*)

HARRIET: What does Violet know about houses? She
  never saw Beaupré –

MAUD: How awful of me – how could I forget? Poor
  Violet, it was all her dreams come true.

HARRIET: Only they didn't. Because Aunt Emma was a
  treacherous old bezum.

MAUD: Harriet!

HARRIET: She promised the world then died intestate –
  isn't that treachery? It would have soured a sweeter
  temper than Violet's. How could she? When I think how
  she'd spoilt the poor wretched girl, inviting her to
  Anglesey every summer while the rest of us had to make
  do with Tenby –

MAUD: Violet was her god-daughter. We weren't.

HARRIET: And what about the damage the old b– Aunt
  Emma did to all of us? Living with Violet was hard
  enough before, but look at her now – a termagant, a –

MAUD: That's enough, Harriet.

HARRIET: I did feel sorry for her, I really did – all her
  glory gone. How silent she turned, no getting a word out
  of her. (*Pause.*) Quite a relief, though, wasn't it?

MAUD: Relief!

HARRIET: You know it was. No more endless prating about
  Aunt Emma's soirées, everyone caring for things of the
  mind – no more of Mr Tyrwhitt, the great authority on
  Locke – no more of their colloquiums – what a word –
  on the Lakeland poets. I feel I've yawned my way
  through every one of those interminable evenings. But to
  Violet it was Parnassus.

MAUD: She needs a home of her own. If only Mr de Lacey
  would propose –

HARRIET: Really, Maud, how unworldly you are. Why
  ever should he? Ask yourself. Why should the only
  bachelor in the neighbourhood marry Violet, who hasn't
  a penny? He knows his price in the market – rates his
  claims highly, does Mr de Lacey. No, there's no husband
  for Violet – unless it's fat old wheezy Mr Lemuel

looking for a wife to paste up his stamp collection.
Imagine! He has some from Borneo.

MAUD: She can't adapt, that's the trouble. She never got
over you being born –

HARRIET: (*Astonished.*) What an extraordinary thing to say.

MAUD: It's true. She was seven – rather plain, and going
through a difficult phase. But she was still Mama's pet.
Then you came along, and you really were a lovely baby
– very jolly. Mama found you diverting from the word
go – played with you all the time. I'm ashamed to say I
did too. Violet was out in the cold.

HARRIET: What nonsense. Why, I was the youngest for
years until Con was born, but I didn't feel my nose out
of joint when she came along. I was rather pleased.

MAUD: (*Quiet.*) We're not talking about you –

HARRIET: (*Not listening.*) Of course she got over it. Really,
Maud, sometimes your ideas are downright silly.

MAUD: Poor Violet –

HARRIET: (*Snorts.*) Poor Violet, indeed. What about me? I
tell you, the day I came back here a widow and saw this
ugly grey barracks of a house heaving itself up at me, I
wished I was dead like Toby. How I've suffered –
(*She picks up a bit of jumble.*)
But of course I never talk about it.
(*MAUD raises her eyes to heaven. HARRIET throws jumble
down in fury.*)
Why oh why can't we live in a nice lively city?
(*MAUD sighs, speaks almost under her breath.*)

MAUD: Oh, Harriet, Harriet –

HARRIET: When we shook the dust of Ireland off our feet
and came to live here because of Papa's foul temper –

MAUD: Please don't talk like that.

HARRIET: Why not? We all know the only reason we left
home was because Papa had quarrelled with every single
friend and relation. By the time we upped sticks he didn't
have even a third cousin left would speak to him. But on

the way here we spent a night in Dublin with Aunt
Grace –

MAUD: My twelfth birthday. She gave me the most
beautiful pair of shoes in the world.

HARRIET: Now there was a city – fun, noise, life – life
everywhere, such life. I laughed whenever I looked out
of the windows in Aunt Grace's house – laughed for
pleasure. Remember the organ grinder with his funny
monkey in a red coat? And the old beggar on the street
corner singing 'O sole mio'? Always something going
on, always life, oh lovely life –

MAUD: Dublin to me means my red shoes. I've never had
anything since I've treasured so – and then I outgrew
them, oh, dear –

HARRIET: I could have been happy for ever in Merrion
Square –
'Had I enough of money, money enough and to spare –
The life for me, the life for me, is a house in the city
square –'
Money, there's the rub. Toby promised he'd take me to
London to see if it's all it's clapped up to be so then of
course he went and died. I'll never see London now. Or
even hear of it.

MAUD: Nonsense –

HARRIET: Oh? Papa takes a newspaper but we're not
allowed to read it. So who kept us in touch with the
outside world? The Granvilles. When they got back from
their last trip to London they told us about Bernard
Shaw's new play. Then The Great Quarrel erupted. So
that's the last news we had of London, and the last we'll
ever have. In ten years' time someone will ask if we
know about some dazzling new spectacle, and we'll say
no, but do let us tell you about the magnificent play by
that clever Mr Shaw which was performed in 1904. *John
Bull's Other Island*, it's called – oh, quite wonderful, I
believe. Such insight. Such characters. What? Written

more since, has he? Do you say so? Well, I'm not surprised. We all knew he had it in him.

(*MAUD is laughing heartily.*)

MAUD: How absurd you are –

HARRIET: (*Shouts.*) We're stuck. Stuck. All news from the outside world came to a grinding halt in 1904.

(*She starts pacing the room.*)

Oh, why weren't we born boys so we could have got away and made our fortunes instead of mouldering here? Then Papa wouldn't have had the awful burden of four daughters – why, he might have been quite cheerful. Oh, why do we have to be poor? I want money – piles and piles of lovely money.

MAUD: What a nasty greedy way to talk. The trouble is, Harriet, you're bored. Why did you give up your drawing? You were so good at it – why not start again?

HARRIET: Draw those wretched hills? All I ever see.

MAUD: No – you used to draw people. They were so observant, your quick sketches – Violet in a fury – Con being – well, being Con – old John with his bleary eye – they were rather unkind, but very clever. And funny. Of course, all three of you can be funny one way or another. I only wish you'd be it more often. You can all make people laugh. I'm not funny, not at all –

(*HARRIET expressionless.*)

– yes, I know, there's no need to say it – but I do like a laugh.

HARRIET: You can hardly blame us for not keeping you in stitches. What is there to feed on? At least we used to have the occasional trip to Shrewsbury – well, it was something. An outing every six months – there's excitement for you. Shops. Cream teas at the Misses Jones's tea rooms – fashions a mere six months behind London – oh, the wild extravagance. But now Mama has given up, we don't even go there. What is there to look forward to?

MAUD: Next week, of course.

(HARRIET looks puzzled.)
Surely you haven't forgotten?
(MAUD laughs.)
Why, it's the sheep-dog trials at Machynlleth, you goose.
(Silence while HARRIET restrains herself from strangling MAUD.)
Harriet?
(HARRIET breathes deeply.)
What's the matter? Did I say something?
(HARRIET speaks through gritted teeth.)

HARRIET: Nothing, absolutely nothing. *(Fury.)* Oh, it's easy for you, you're a saint – no one else could be happy in this dead and alive place.

MAUD: How blind and ungrateful you are. Open your eyes. Look at the trees, and the waterfalls, and the shadows chasing over the hills. The hand of God is everywhere.

HARRIET: *(Impatient.)* No doubt.

MAUD: When I climb the Foel and reach the uplands, I'm as happy as anyone could be in this world.

HARRIET: But there's nothing there.

MAUD: Nothing. Only the odd sheep's bone – short grass and the wind asking why you've come. Nothing. But up there I think even you would be aware of the very presence of God.

HARRIET: Really? I must go and have a look. *(Cross.)* There's no merit in your goodness, you know. You have your religion, and your trees and mountains and laughing brooks and – and rippling rivulets – all that insalubrious nature you enthuse over – you have everything you want.

MAUD: How can you say that when Con is so ill? And when you and Violet fill the house with your discontent –

HARRIET: I'm not like Violet. Not at all.

MAUD: – and Con gets upset over nothing – her terrible ups and downs are very wearing, not her fault, but they

are. And every day – just think of it, Harriet, every
single day – you complain because we don't live in a
city. And Mama – and Papa – oh dear. (*Snorts.*) All I
want, indeed. (*Pause.*) The only bright spot on the
horizon is Mr Rudd.

HARRIET: That dull little man? What are you talking
about?

MAUD: He can't take his eyes off Con.

HARRIET: What rubbish. How many times has he seen
her? Once? Twice? Why, he's only been in the district
three weeks, and now he's settled his aunt's estate he'll be
off again. He's been to the house twice –

MAUD: Five times.

HARRIET: But only because Papa owns the shooting rights
and there were oh, I don't know – things to sign –

MAUD: He only needed to come once. The other times it
was an excuse. If you'd seen him watching Con –

HARRIET: Control your spinster's imagination, do. It's
nonsense. In any case, his grandparents made boots in
Northampton. We all know Mr Rudd has money, but
Papa would not overlook the boots for any amount. If it
comes to that, neither would I.

MAUD: It has nothing to do with you. Or me. He's rich.
He could take her away to the sun. It might save her. It's
her one hope, and you are not to interfere. It's between
the two of them and God.

HARRIET: Oh, once you start bringing God into it there's
no arguing with you. Always on your side, isn't he? Very
selfish, the way you monopolise him – the rest of us
don't get a look in. (*Pause.*) Con won't encourage Mr
Rudd. She knows what's due to herself and to the rest
of us.

MAUD: And why should we look down on Mr Rudd?

HARRIET: Really, Maud. Remember who we are.

MAUD: Ah. You think because Papa is the younger son of a
younger son of a drunken Irish marquess who died from
a cracked skull when he slipped dancing a reel – on the

dining table, naturally – with his favourite pig that we have cause for self-congratulation. Does it raise us so high in the eyes of God?

HARRIET: You say the most shocking things, Maud, in that quiet little voice of yours. I'm quite amazed sometimes. Really, I don't know where you get your ideas from. You seem to have no proper pride.

(*Enter VIOLET.*)

VIOLET: Who's taken my green silk scarf?

HARRIET: Take something of yours? Which of us would dare? And it's certainly not me, I hate green –

VIOLET: Someone did.

HARRIET: – and that acid monstrosity of yours makes me feel ill.

(*VIOLET goes to fireplace, rings bell violently.*)

Such a bilious shade it gives your face. And if anyone took it –

VIOLET: I tell you someone took it. Someone took it.

HARRIET: – it certainly wasn't one of us. We don't love you enough to want your ugly scarf as a keepsake.

(*Sudden shriek of laughter.*)

Perhaps Mr de Lacey stole it as a love token – why, Violet, how you glare.

(*VIOLET rings the bell even more violently.*)

MAUD: Please don't start. Either of you. It's so exhausting.

HARRIET: You see? You're exhausting Maud.

(*The door bursts open and HILDA comes in, bringing with her a gust of anger, passion and energy. She is Welsh; even when her words are civil her looks are full of resentment, which is the key-stone of her existence. She looks at once at VIOLET; it is clear it is always she who rings.*)

HILDA: Yes, Miss Violet.

VIOLET: You took your time, Hilda.

HILDA: I was doing the washing, Miss Violet. I had to dry my hands. Then I ran up the stairs as fast as I could, but my bad leg is tiresome today. It –

VIOLET: (*Interrupting.*) Where is my green scarf? You know I won't have my things moved.

HILDA: It's in the hall where you left it.

VIOLET: I left it in my room.

HILDA: You threw it down in the hall when you came in yesterday. On the floor. I picked it up and folded it so it was tidy. The Major doesn't like to see things on the floor, only what he throws there himself.

VIOLET: That will do. You may go.

HILDA: There's nothing else you'd like me to do now I'm up here? Nothing to be fetched from your bedroom? It would save time if I could get it now, rather than you ring again just when I've got downstairs, and my leg will slow me up you see, which will be irritating for you –

VIOLET: Hilda. You may go.

HILDA: Thank you, Miss Violet. Thank you.

(*She goes. HARRIET sits back and contemplates VIOLET.*)

HARRIET: Now you've made a perfect fool of yourself I hope you're satisfied. Accusing us of taking your ugly scarf –

MAUD: Harriet, please, please don't make Violet rise.

VIOLET: Rise? You talk as though I were a sea monster –

HARRIET: No, a land monster – a house monster – at the sight of you peace and concord turn on their heels and skeddadle like bats out of hell –

(*VIOLET opens her mouth to strike back; gently MAUD takes her arm.*)

MAUD: All Harriet means is that life might be more peaceful if you were less determined to hate us all. We know you'd prefer not to be living with the rest of us, but there is, after all, no chance of escape. So we might as well make the best of it.

HARRIET: Oh, Violet thinks Mr de Lacey will come for her, a white knight on a black charger, and carry her off – stop wobbling those eyebrows at me – why should we be nice to you? When were you last nice to any of us?

(The door opens again and a bent little old woman in black comes in. She has a slight St Vitus's dance, a perpetual twitch. MAUD gets up at once, HARRIET more slowly; VIOLET is already standing.)

ALL: Good morning, Mama.

(MRS ROSS-MARTIN ignores them, speaks only to herself.)

MRS ROSS-MARTIN: Where did I put it? Lost again, oh, dear – where is it?

(MAUD goes to her, very kindly.)

MAUD: Where is what, Mama?

MRS ROSS-MARTIN: When the shouting starts it gets lost – yes, it happens when the shouting starts –
(She goes distractedly to a drawer, pulls it open.)
No, it's not there, of course not, it never is –
(She slams drawer shut.)
Oh dear, oh dear, the shouting's got into my head –
(She goes out, shaking and muttering. The three stand stock-still, listening anxiously. Long pause.)

VIOLET: She imagined it –
(They are all three momentarily united; stand rigid, listening. Then slowly they begin to relax, when a sudden low throated roaring from outside, words indistinguishable. They all three rush together, united for once. HARRIET seizes a chair and holds it in front of them.)

MAUD: Put it down.

HARRIET: I won't.

MAUD: He's never hit us –

HARRIET: It makes me feel safer – I shake so when he looms over us and roars –

VIOLET: You should be used to it.

HARRIET: I'm not. I never will be.

MAUD: Put it down, Harriet. If you pick up a stone when a dog barks, it feels your fear.

HARRIET: Papa lacks the sensitivity of a dog.
(The roaring stops and they stand stock-still, straining, listening. Total silence. Suddenly it begins again, but much nearer. Dies down. Silence.)

MAUD: God is our hope and strength: a very present help
  in trouble.

HARRIET: Oh, really, Maud, what a time to start praying –

MAUD: Therefore will we not fear though the earth be
  moved: and though the hills be carried into the midst of
  the sea.
  (*The roaring stops.*)
  Though the waters thereof rage and swell:
  (*Roaring starts, but much further off. Sound of tremendously
  loudly slammed door, followed by pony and trap driving away.*)
  – and though the mountains shake at the tempest of the
  same. Be still then and know that I am God –
  (*They all breathe deeply. HARRIET turns to MAUD.*)

HARRIET: Well done, Maud. God's saved us – with your
  help, of course, what would He do without you?
  (*MAUD looks at her.*)
  I'm sorry, I'm sorry –

VIOLET: Anyhow, he's gone –

HARRIET: A whole day's peace –
  (*She stretches luxuriously.*)
  It almost makes one fond of Violet.
  (*She catches VIOLET's eye.*)

VIOLET: Keep your fondness for your neglected children,
  left to the mercies of that ignorant girl all day. They're a
  disgrace – dirty frocks – runny noses –

MAUD: Stop it – both of you.

HARRIET: She started it.
  (*Turns to VIOLET.*)
  If only Mr de Lacey would whisk you off and marry you,
  how peaceful the rest of us would live. But you'll never
  bring him to book, you haven't the skill.
  (*MAUD is looking from one to the other in anguish. Tries to
  interrupt, but they're at it.*)

VIOLET: How coarse your mind is. I wonder where you
  got it from?

HARRIET: It is strange, isn't it, how different traits in a
  family show themselves? I watch you at meals and

wonder where your greed came from. Don't you find Violet's greed remarkable, Maud?

(*MAUD puts her hands over her ears.*)

Such stamina she shows. Such admirable all-round virtuosity. Spring lamb, roast beef, steak and kidney pudding – she's always avid for more. First into the trough, queen of the second helpings. And cream, we like a little cream, don't we? I wonder where it all goes, she's not fat, after all. And I do admire, Violet, the delicacy with which you wipe your lips as though you'd toyed with the merest trifle. A little dab here, a little dab there –

VIOLET: What a pity Toby wasn't more provident. Then you wouldn't have had to come crawling back begging for bread for yourself and your unfortunate children, and the necessity for watching me would not have arisen.

MAUD: Oh, why – why do you hurt each other so?

(*HARRIET gets up. She and VIOLET look at each other. MAUD goes to HARRIET, glaring at VIOLET. HARRIET speaks matter of factly.*)

HARRIET: You've turned the air as cold as your heart.

(*She goes, shutting the door quietly behind her.*)

MAUD: How could you?

VIOLET: She began it.

(*She speaks in sudden fury.*)

She's intolerable – everything she does grates on me – she's a sore tooth. And her conceit – Beaupré, indeed – why, everyone knows the place is a crumbling ruin – barn owls nesting in the roof. If she'd ever seen Glynn Abbot – good heavens, is she the only one whose hopes were dashed? Does she ever think of me?

MAUD: We're all very sorry Aunt Emma forgot to make a will. But we've been sorry now for a long time –

VIOLET: Five years. Three months. Ten days.

MAUD: – and our initial sympathy has worn off. We can't go on being sorry for ever. It's over.

VIOLET: Over? I remember every hour of the day.

MAUD: If only you could learn to adapt. Stop eating your
life away.

VIOLET: But the unfairness – you saw her letter. You saw it.
I was her heir. I should be sitting by my own hearth
running my own household. Glynn Abbot was mine. It
was promised.

MAUD: It's not cosmic, Violet. You've lost an agreeable
house, that's all.

VIOLET: Agreeable! The best house on the island – and the
perfect setting for the intellectual life we led. I suppose
there was never a more elegant salon than Aunt Emma's
– her knowledge of the English poets was unrivalled –
(*MAUD sighs and turns back to sorting jumble.*)
At Glynn Abbot we cared for things of the mind. If you
could have heard Mr Tyrwhitt, the great authority on
Locke –

MAUD: Look outwards, Violet, and up to God. There is no
other salvation. You're not the only one whose hopes
have been dashed. And it's not as though you've had the
worst of it. Think of Con, so ill, and poor Harriet – she
lost her husband, her life –

VIOLET: And didn't I? Where's the life Aunt Emma
promised me? I was the only person fit to tend the
sacred flame of the salon she'd created. She said so. It
was settled. But she forgot, didn't she, forgot to make her
will, so the house went to her stupid sister who never
read a book and it's as though that wonderful temple of
the mind had never existed. How could she do it to me?
How could she hurt me so?

MAUD: I don't expect she meant to. People do forget
things, after all.

VIOLET: I can't even read Tennyson's poems any more. I
used to read them with her. Since she betrayed me
they're meaningless. She's broken my life.

MAUD: Accept God's will –
(*VIOLET makes furious movement.*)

God's will, Violet. God's will. Bury Glynn Abbot and come alive again. And try to be a little nicer to the rest of us – we might even enjoy each other's company. We have in the past. Why, you used to make me laugh – quite a lot. And we are family, after all –

VIOLET: Not me. I'm no part of this family.

(*Stands glaring at MAUD.*)

The first time I went to Glynn Abbot Aunt Emma looked at me as I came through the door and said 'Why, you're not a Ross-Martin. You're a Holroyd.' I was twelve years old. From that moment I knew I belonged there. I'm a Holroyd – a different breed to the rest of you. I've been in the wrong family all my life.

(*CON has come in and is standing listening, unnoticed. She is about 25. Like HARRIET and VIOLET, she is passionate, noisy, arrogant and self-centred, but she is more hopeful and laughs easily. She is much the best looking of the sisters, but she is pale and looks very ill. She dresses very well; would look good in anything. She sees VIOLET, and makes the sign of the evil eye, with some violence. VIOLET has her back turned, and doesn't see, but MAUD does, and is puzzled.*)

MAUD: Con – what are you doing? What –?

(*CON takes no notice; goes to the bell and rings it; looks at pile of jumble.*)

CON: What odd possessions we've had, hidden away – kept them very quiet from each other, haven't we?

(*Holds up a puce blouse.*)

I suppose this is Violet's.

(*She drops it with a fastidious shudder.*)

The only one of us to chose her colours entirely by ear.

(*VIOLET throws herself angrily into a chair; picks up a book; reads.*)

MAUD: And where is your contribution, Con?

(*CON turns pile over with her foot.*)

CON: I'm afraid I have nothing grotesque enough to blend in with – all that –

(*She looks round the room.*)

Couldn't we give all these depressing paintings?

MAUD: Don't be silly. They came from Papa's home.

CON: Ah. Family throw-outs. Yet another drawback of being a younger son –
(*She walks round them.*)
Dead pheasants. Ugh. Who would have thought the little birds had so much blood in them? Death of the boar. Death of a gaffed salmon. Death of the fox. Death, doom, and destruction –
(*Enter HILDA.*)
– just Papa's cup of tea. Oh, Hilda, have you seen –

HILDA: Yes, Miss Violet.

VIOLET: I didn't ring.

HILDA: I'm sorry, Miss Violet, but it always is you, you see. So of course I thought it would be you this time.

CON: I rang, Hilda.

HILDA: So when I heard the bell I thought, there, perhaps Miss Violet's lost her gloves again. Or perhaps she wants me to go upstairs and fetch her needle. Like she did yesterday.

CON: Hilda, I've lost my book.

HILDA: 'That'll be Miss Violet needing something,' I said to John, as I dried my hands again, and John said –
(*VIOLET leaves the room in a fury.*)

CON: Have you seen it? It has a blue cover with roses swirling all over it in gold.
(*MAUD walks over to a pile of books; picks one out which she drops in CON's lap.*)
Oh, Maud, how clever you are. I'm sorry I called you for nothing, Hilda.

HILDA: Thank you, Miss Con –
(*She goes.*)

MAUD: What did you do when Violet came in? You made a sort of gesture – you looked horrid.

CON: I made the sign of the evil eye. To protect myself.

MAUD: Con! How can you? She's your sister –

CON: Bizarre, isn't it?

MAUD: It was graceless of you. And I was feeling so sorry
 for her –
CON: Sorry! Were you now.
MAUD: She can't adapt, you see. It makes her so unhappy –
 (*CON speaks in sudden fury.*)
CON: I don't want to hear her name. I don't want to think
 about her.
 (*MAUD looks at her anxiously.*)
MAUD: Con. Don't start. I won't mention her again. Just be
 still now –
 (*MAUD goes back to sorting. CON sits, opens book, finds
 place. Reads.*)
CON: I must find out what happens to Lord Fotheringham.
 He's trussed up like a chicken in a rat-filled dungeon –
 no breaking out of those chains. I can hardly leave him
 there while you go keening over Violet's wrongs.
MAUD: If we treated her better, she might respond to
 kindness –
 (*CON snorts. She reads. Silence. Suddenly gasps in fury.*)
CON: He's burst his bonds. But we were told on page 72 it
 was impossible. And here he is on page 75 leaping about
 like a two year old – if ever there was a cheat in this
 world –
 (*Throws down book, suddenly rushes at MAUD in fury, shakes
 her.*)
 We're to be kind to her, are we? Kind!
 (*MAUD looks at her, aghast.*)
 She's done for me.
 (*She picks book up, shuts it properly, and puts it down.*)
 Yesterday Mr Rudd came to propose. He'd just managed
 to get to the point – and oh, the time it took – when
 Violet came in. And sat. She knew what she was doing –
 there are no accidents in Violet's behaviour. Her sandy
 eyebrows went up and down, and the silences grew
 longer, until Mr Rudd gave up and left. When he'd gone,
 she looked at me. Then she left the room, smiling to
 herself. A good morning's work, she was thinking.

(*Throws herself in a chair.*)
She's killed me as surely as if she'd stuck a knife in my heart.

MAUD: No – she wouldn't –

CON: Oh? She knows if I stay here I shall die. Only two months ago I could still walk up the hills. And look at me now, I can hardly trail round the shrubberies. Mr Rudd is rich. He could have taken me away to the sun, and I would have got better – I think. Yes. I'm sure I would have got better. He was my one chance. And Violet's put a stop to it. She's killed me, Maud. As she meant to.

MAUD: He'll come again –

CON: No. He leaves tomorrow.

MAUD: But he'll be back – in a few months, perhaps –

CON: What use to me when I'm under the sod? I tell you, Maud, I shudder now when we walk through that dank churchyard –
(*Turns to MAUD, urgent.*)
You know the corner near the old yew – where the sun comes. Make them put me there. If you let them put me anywhere else I'll haunt you, Maud. I promise. I'll give you no rest –
(*HILDA comes in.*)

HILDA: A note for you, Miss Con –
(*She hands it over. CON looks at the writing.*)
The boy said it didn't need an answer.

CON: Thank you, Hilda –
(*HILDA goes. CON collapses into chair.*)
It's from him.
(*She starts coughing and puts her handkerchief to her mouth. She looks at it briefly then puts it away quickly. Reads note. Clutches MAUD.*)
Maud – there's hope – oh, I don't believe it – hope –
(*She looks at note.*)
He wants to see me before he goes. He's coming tomorrow at eleven. Hope, Maud – I'm going to live –

(*Gets up, business-like.*)
But it's last chance. He must propose tomorrow, and –
oh, lor, in this room – the rain won't stop just because we
want to walk in the garden. And Violet – if she has an
inkling she'll come and outsit him – it'll be like last
time. Maud. You must keep her out if you have to tie her
in the airing cupboard and sit on her. Can you do it?

MAUD: I don't know. I can try.

CON: You must. You must help me – promise you'll help
me –

(*There is a silence. When MAUD assents, it is with reluctance.*)

MAUD: I suppose so – yes. All right. I'll help you – but –

CON: If she comes in here you must drag her out by the
hairs of her head. And Harriet must help. Oh, if only he
weren't so shy – the least thing could scare him off –

MAUD: Are you sure – really sure – you want to marry
him?

CON: Maud. I can hear people talking in a year or two's
time. 'There were four of them, weren't there? And then
one of them took to the coughing and died – quite
young, too, so sad –' Mr Rudd can keep me out of the
grave. I want to live. I want to be old and jolly and fat
and rich. I want splendid clothes and cheerful friends
who make me laugh – I want to laugh for lightness of
heart like the Granvilles laugh – ah, Maud, don't look so
shocked and sad –

MAUD: You're so pretty, Con. You should have the pick of
the world, not have to go angling for Mr Rudd –

CON: He's not the husband I dreamt of when I was 17. But
I'm 25 and near death, and there's no rush of suitors to
the door. I've come to terms and so must you. Think of
the compensations. Life, to begin with, nothing wrong
with that.

MAUD: Poor Mr Rudd –

CON: And I'll have a fine elegant house in London – you
shall make your home with us. He lives in Rutland Gate.
Do you suppose it's smart? It sounds rather countrified.

What a delightful time you and I will have when I'm a
brisk married woman living in London –

MAUD: Poor Mr Rudd –

CON: Oh, do stop saying Poor Mr Rudd.

MAUD: And he's so shy he might sit here tongue-tied even
if you were uninterrupted –

CON: No. I can do it. Look – Mr Rudd comes in. I am
disposed on this sofa. I look up, languishing, and give
him my hand, which remains in his. I look at him with
passionate interest – am I doing well?

MAUD: Over-eager. And rather vulgar.

(*CON gives exclamation of impatience.*)

CON: 'Mr Rudd, we hear you are leaving us –' languish,
languish, tears – no, one tear, unshed, but brimming in
the eye – this eye –

MAUD: You can't cry to order.

CON: When I think of myself lying underground, which
will be the case very soon unless Mr Rudd offers, I can
not only cry to order, I can do it quite naturally. None of
that, now, where was I? 'Your leaving, Mr Rudd, will
cause a great gap in our little society. You will be sorely
missed –' now, under my breath as though not meaning
to be heard – 'at least by one.' And then I let the tear
well over onto our joined hands. Then I lift my head and
look straight at him and if you say 'Poor Mr Rudd' again
I'll hit you, Maud –

MAUD: Whatever would Violet say to such behaviour?

CON: I'll adopt behaviour again when I'm safely married.
At the minute I can't afford it.

(*She gets up and walks up and down the room, stops.*)
I knew I was heading for the dark at a rate of knots
when I noticed that on a bad day getting dressed took
half an hour, and then all I wanted to do was go back to
bed. Oh, I knew I was dying, all right. But I didn't care,
you know. Not a jot.

MAUD: Of course you must have cared, don't be
ridiculous.

CON: Why on earth should I? Think of our life – our daily ritual dance between here and the dining room. The dining room, ugh. Hideous dark furniture – bog oak, of course – and heavy – in my state I can hardly move my chair. And crimson walls covered with engravings of memorable moments from Roman history. Three times a day, during those endless silent meals, I sit opposite Julius Caesar being stabbed to the heart. He looks surprised, and who can blame him? Stoical, though. Putting a good face on it. On death. Yes. And while Julius Caesar and I commune wordlessly – we've grown quite close over the years – John, tipsy as usual, spills gravy on our dresses and breathes whisky fumes over us as he hands us the potatoes. After dinner we come back here. Papa has drunk himself into a state of insensibility. And then the nightmares attack him, and he cries out in his sleep about the horrors he saw as a child in County Mayo – then he wakes and forces us to sing dismal songs about young love. And this happens every single day; in these rooms we pass our life. And there is no hope of escape. I tell you, Maud, our lives are not up to snuff.

MAUD: This world is only a shadow, Con.

CON: Ah, stuff – (*Pause.*) I'm sorry, Maud, I'm sorry. But I was not only resigned to dying – I was relieved. Ready and waiting. Until the day I nearly got killed.

MAUD: What? You never told me.

CON: I was in the lane near Owen's farm – so narrow you can't get three people abreast. Suddenly I heard a great noise, and there coming at me was a runaway horse, trailing a cart behind him, filling the lane. There wasn't room to swing a cockroach. And when I saw the ugly brute heading straight for me, I did a leap I never would have thought possible. I was up the bank and clinging to an ash tree in less time than I could think it. And the horse went on crashing down the hill, but I went on clinging to the branch, suspended in air.

MAUD: Why did you never tell me?

CON: And as I hung I heard myself shouting – 'I'm alive!'
How happy I was – I felt so cheerful – even started
singing. All this joy simply because I was alive. So then,
of course, I knew I did care, oh, how I cared – and death
was terrible. And I let go of the branch and sat in the
lane, kicking the ground in rage – oh, what a fury I was
in. Because there was no hope of getting away to the sun
and I'd be dead within months.

MAUD: How could you not tell me?

CON: I had other things on my mind. Because on that very
afternoon Mr Rudd came to the house for the first time,
and I saw him looking at me, and I knew God had
spoken.

MAUD: (*Quiet.*) That's blasphemy, Con.

CON: And now he's coming, carrying my life in the palm
of his hand. Oh, how am I to get through the night? I
shan't sleep, I'll look terrible when he comes, those awful
circles I get round the eyes – he'll be off – what shall I
wear? My blue? Or my pale grey – a good fit, the grey,
yes, a very good fit – what's the matter?

MAUD: Stop it! Stop it!
(*CON looks at her in amazement.*)
It's obscene – inhuman. You're talking as though he was
a lover when you don't give a fig for him –
(*Silence.*)
Have you the slightest regard for this man you're so
passionately set on marrying? No, you have not. To you
he's just a prop – another ash tree. No one deserves to be
treated with such lack of humanity. He has feelings. He
has a soul.
(*CON looks shattered.*)

CON: But you'll help me. You promised. You always keep
your word.

MAUD: I will help you, God forgive me. As best I can.
But you must know what a sin you're committing. And
admit it.
(*Silence.*)

CON: (*Very soft.*) I do know. I admit it. May God forgive us both.

TWO

The same room, evening of the same day. The pile of clothes has gone from the floor. The curtains are drawn and the lamps are lit. MAJOR ROSS-MARTIN is slumped, dozing, in the large chair on one side of the fire. He is about to fall into a heavy sleep, but is not quite off yet – occasionally turns and thrashes about. He is a very large man in his sixties, with drooping moustaches and whiskers, vacant but choleric blue eyes and an enormous hooked nose. His mouth is sad, small, and indeterminate. His evening clothes are green with age. MRS ROSS-MARTIN is in the rocking chair, rocking backwards and forwards – but with a straight back – and dozing. MAUD and CON are sitting on the sofa: MAUD is reading; CON has needlework, but keeps throwing it down and fidgeting.

CON: Maud –
> (*MAUD goes on reading. CON waits hopefully, but MAUD goes on reading. Silence.*)
> Maud!
> (*MAUD comes to reluctantly, but keeps a finger in her book.*)
> Why does the dining room have such hideous wallpaper?
> Crimson – ugh.

MAUD: Why ask now? You've seen it every day of your life.

CON: So I've never noticed it. But now Mr Rudd and the tomb are competing for me, I'm off – one way or another. And I find myself looking at things as though I'd never seen them before. This evening I looked at the dining room walls.

MAUD: Crimson is supposed to encourage the appetite.
> (*Opens her book and starts reading.*)

CON: Oh. (*She broods.*) In Violet's case it does a pretty good job, doesn't it?
> (*Silence. CON turns to MAUD, urgent.*)
> Doesn't it? Answer me – talk to me –
> (*MAUD puts her book down, looks up, surprised.*)

183

To blazes with the walls, they can be puce with orange spots for all I care – I'm just trying to stop my mind flying about – it keeps taking off – talk to me, please – help me –

(*Snore from MAJOR ROSS-MARTIN. CON looks at him, grim.*)

I see Papa has drunk himself into his usual state of insensibility –

MAUD: Shh!

CON: Oh, rubbish, shh indeed. Why should I shh? He's dead to the world – until the nightmares come out of his childhood and scream at him. But they happened sixty years ago, why can't he get over them? People do get over things. What's wrong with him?

(*She gets up, goes over and examines her father closely.*)

MAUD: Come back – what are you thinking of?

(*CON stands over her father.*)

CON: I want a good look at him. Him – and the dining room walls – and anything else that takes my fancy.

(*She examines him carefully. Shakes her head.*)

Nothing there. Just a drunken, bullying, improvident old tyrant who cries out in his sleep about the famine –

(*MAUD gasps. MAJOR ROSS-MARTIN shifts, settles. CON stands looking at him.*)

Colonel Granville talks to his children in the evening, did you know? Think of it – a father who talks to his children –

(*Snarls at her father.*)

Why can't you be like Colonel Granville?

MAUD: Con! How can you?

(*CON comes back to her chair.*)

CON: Don't fuss – he's buried in sleep.

(*CON watches both her parents. MAJOR ROSS-MARTIN has settled, gives an occasional snore. MRS ROSS-MARTIN rocks steadily. CON stifles a hysterical laugh.*)

'Grow old along with me

The best is yet to be –'

MAUD: You're graceless, Con. Whatever you feel, you
should show respect for your parents.
(*She glares at CON and goes firmly back to her book. CON
tries her needlework, throws it down.*)
CON: Talk to me. I tell you my mind keeps flying about –
giving off sparks – I can't anchor it –
(*With a sigh, MAUD puts down her book.*)
Make me laugh – try, can't you? Are there jokes in your
book? You know if I don't laugh I get ill, so why don't
you help? What are you reading?
MAUD: *King Lear.*
(*Silence.*)
CON: *King Lear.*
(*Silence.*)
Sometimes, Maud, you go too far.
(*She turns on MAUD in a fury.*)
Put it down – put it down and keep me sane. I don't
know how to get through to tomorrow – anchor me –
keep me safe –
(*MAUD sighs, picks up CON's work.*)
MAUD: What are you thinking of? You've embroidered that
rose in blue.
CON: 'Blue were her eyes as the fairy flax –' what poem is
that? It doesn't make sense, no sense –
MAUD: 'Yellow her hair as the fairy flax,' silly –
CON: Ah. Or perhaps 'Yellow her eyes as the fairy flax,'
that's more striking – lions have yellow eyes, don't they?
And they glow in the dark. Or is it tigers? Oh, yellow
eyes would be irresistible – who wouldn't swoon for a
man who came courting with burning yellow eyes – why,
you'd be the envy of the neighbourhood. Whatever
would the Misses Unwin say if it happened to them?
They'd be overcome entirely –
MAUD: Your hands are shaking. You've worn yourself out.
CON: Like the Misses Unwin at the thought of yellow eyes.
'We had a charming picnic with our friend Mr
Hirosimus – he has yellow eyes, you know.' 'I'm so sorry

we cannot come to your At Home, Mrs Golightly –
we're expecting our amusing acquaintance with the
yellow eyes –'

MAUD: Go to bed.

CON: No – no –

MAUD: I'll make your excuses when Papa wakes up – say
you were tired –

CON: I won't go to bed – it's not bedtime – I won't go
before bedtime. How could I sleep? When he's coming
tomorrow? What? Go to bed and toss and turn before I
have to? How cruel you are.

(*MAJOR ROSS-MARTIN gives a particularly loud snort in
his sleep. MRS ROSS-MARTIN stops rocking; looks anxiously
at him, but he settles down again. She begins rocking again,
fast at first, then back to her usual pace. CON looks at her
parents, frowning.*)

Why did Mama marry Papa? He was handsome, I
suppose, in his uniform. Full of fire – hope –

(*She shivers.*)

Fire. Hope. And where's the dashing young subaltern she
saw? There's no sign of him – no trace.

(*Speaks directly to her father.*)

Where have you hidden him? Is he in there somewhere
trying to get out? Or did you bury him? In which case,
did he die of natural causes? Or perhaps you murdered
him. I wouldn't put it past you.

(*MAUD looks at her in bewilderment.*)

MAUD: Come and sit down – you're out of your mind –

CON: I'm not. It's like I said – I've started noticing things.

(*Slowly she goes back to sofa, casting glances at her father.
She sits; looks at her mother, who is rocking steadily.*)

CON: Mama was always dancing, did you know? Annie
told me when she was a girl her feet were as light as her
heart. And there she sits rocking in a world of her own.
Did she go there to get away from Papa? Is it to end up
like her I'm trying to stay alive? (*Louder.*) Why bother? I
might as well die now –

MAUD: Hush – you'd be better off in bed, I know you would.

CON: Ah, would I now. Look at them, Maud. Both of them. If I thought that was the way every hope ended, the game would not be worth the candle. That's the question, isn't it? Is the game worth the candle? Come along, answer me. You should know these things, you're older than me. So is the game –

(*MAJOR ROSS-MARTIN turns violently in his sleep; shouts out without waking.*)

MAJOR ROSS-MARTIN: No more soup –

(*CON looks at her father, scowls.*)

CON: Back in County Mayo, are you? Well don't ask me to join you, I'm sick of the wretched place – want no part of it. It has nothing to do with us, we weren't even born. Who cares for Ireland's sufferings and her glum lugubrious past? Certainly not me. And I resent them being forced down my throat every evening in this ham-fisted manner. How dare they intrude on my life? Such self-pity. I don't give a fig for Ireland's woes and the more they're paraded in front of me the less I care. Tirra lirra to the lot of them.

(*Does a dance step under her father's nose.*)

For two pins I'd dance a fandango.

MAUD: Ssh – ssh –

CON: Stop telling me to shh – I won't. Isn't it bad enough to pass our days in this dreary place without the Shan Van Vocht looming over us every evening? Come back to Erin? Not if I can help it. The land of my birth can get along without me, thank you very much. Oh, Maud, is this the way to pass our life? Sitting here chatting idly while Mama rocks away and Papa slumps there in hell?

(*MAJOR ROSS-MARTIN stirs in his sleep, mutters. CON hisses at him.*)

It's over – it happened sixty years ago – it's over, can't you understand?

MAUD: But it's not over. Not for him. Those poor famished figures crawling up the drive for food are more real than we are. We're in the shadow, the ghosts in his world. We don't enter his mind; we're not even on the edge of his sight. I suppose he sees the birds he shoots, the foxes he hunts. But he doesn't see us.

CON: Perhaps one evening those terrible live ghosts will burst in and join us – quite a party, that will be. Will we dance a jig with the famished skeletons? Oh – I forgot. I won't be here. Or perhaps I'll be one of them. If I am you must dance with me.

(*She leans towards MAUD, menacing.*)

I'll ask you, Maud. I promise.

(*MAJOR ROSS-MARTIN again turns violently; speaks without waking.*)

MAJOR ROSS-MARTIN: Seamus – old Seamus –

MAUD: You should feel pity for him. He's never got over the terrible sights he saw as a child. He fills his life with violent exercise to keep them at bay, but his days in the saddle are haunted by those white famished faces, voices shrieking reproaches on the wind –

CON: Really, Maud. Celtic twilight? From you? Pull yourself together.

MAJOR ROSS-MARTIN: Mother – he can't walk – Seamus –

CON: Oh, to blazes with your old famine – what were we talking about? Games – candles – yellow eyes, was it? Oh, help, Maud – help – help me hang on to my mind – oh, I can't keep still, can't keep –

MAUD: Stop working yourself into such a state. It's very self-indulgent, and if you don't take a grip you'll get a fever. Then you won't be able to get up tomorrow. End of Mr Rudd.

CON: 'And it's oh, dear, what will become of me,
Oh, dear, what will become of me,
Oh, dear, what will become of me –'
(*Pause.*)

– lying beneath the cold ground –
(*Throws herself onto sofa onto MAUD, who holds her.*)
Oh, Maud, I can't think, I can't think – why is this
happening to me? I'm the youngest, I shouldn't be ill –
why isn't it Harriet, she's had her life – or Violet, who'd
miss Violet –
(*The door opens, silently, and VIOLET comes in, carrying a
book. She closes the door without a sound, and stands looking
at MAUD and CON, silent, motionless. CON suddenly
stiffens, shivers; speaks without looking round.*)
She's here –
(*MAUD looks round, sees VIOLET, who glides silently to a
chair as far away as possible. MAUD holds CON tighter.*)
Keep her away from me – keep her away –

MAUD: Pull yourself together – try now, do –

CON: I am trying – but I'm trembling so – what's she
doing?

MAUD: She's reading the book Mr de Lacey lent her – the
Confessions of St Augustine –

CON: And smiling is she? The horrid way she does?
(*She looks furtively at VIOLET, then looks away hastily.*)
She's planning something wicked – hiding behind St
Augustine's skirts and planning evil in his shadow –

MAUD: Stop it, Con. Control your mind.

CON: (*Wild.*) Then help me hang on to it – what am I to do
with this ridiculous fluster? Dance a jig? Run over the
mountains in the rain? Help me –
(*HARRIET comes in, slams the door noisily.*)

HARRIET: What a terrible day I've had –
(*She starts towards CON and MAUD, but stops as her father
cries out in his sleep.*)

MAJOR ROSS-MARTIN: Why – why is he crawling?
(*HARRIET looks at him.*)

HARRIET: The nightmares have started early tonight.
(*Snorts.*) Must be something he ate.

MAJOR ROSS-MARTIN: Walk – Seamus – stand up –
(*HARRIET stands looking at him.*)

HARRIET: Strange, isn't it? During the day Ireland might not exist. He never mentions the wretched place –
(From now on MAJOR ROSS-MARTIN is muttering to himself, generally inaudible; but at intervals the words 'No more soup' are heard.)
But of course he never mentions anything, does he? Just roars for what he wants –
(She hurls herself into a chair next to MAUD.)
– and bellows when things displease him – where was I?

MAUD: Having a terrible day.

HARRIET: Oh, it was, it was. Ulick had earache. You're so lucky, both of you, nothing to do all day but enjoy yourselves – only yourselves to please. You don't know what it's like to have children and feel their pain. Poor little boy – how I suffered. Being a widow doesn't suit me, that's the trouble. It's not my style – it's ridiculous, I feel such a fool – oh, his crying went straight through me – you can't imagine what my day was like –

MAUD: I'm sure you'll tell us. At considerable length.

HARRIET: *(Hurt.)* You're doing it again, Maud – speaking in that horrid tone. I wish you wouldn't – it makes me unhappy. Don't you care about your nephew?

CON: *(Fury.)* You weren't talking about him. You were wallowing in your own foetid emotions. Ulick was a passing footnote – barely rated a mention.
(HARRIET looks at CON in surprise.)

HARRIET: You're very sour this evening. What's the matter? And why have you embroidered that rose in blue? It looks absurd.

CON: *(Flustered.)* Leave me alone, do –

HARRIET: And you're shaking. What's wrong with you? And why is Violet looking so pleased with herself – sitting there reading – *(Pause.)* No. She's not reading, is she? Just – sitting.
(She watches VIOLET, who appears oblivious. CON keeps her head down and sews wildly.)

She's eaten someone. Or she's about to. Yes. She's
planning destruction.
(*HARRIET gets up, speaks briskly.*)
I'll wake her up. Make her hiss –
(*CON throws down her sewing, sits shaking.*)
CON: Please, Harriet, don't – not tonight – don't upset
her –
HARRIET: What on earth is the matter? You enjoy baiting
Violet as much as I do. It's something we have in
common – reminds us we're sisters –
(*CON takes her arm to stop her; HARRIET frees herself.*)
I need a bit of fun – such a day as I've had –
(*HARRIET leaves them; CON and MAUD watch anxiously
as she goes and sits down by VIOLET and starts whispering
in her ear. VIOLET takes no notice, gives no sign she is
listening, but her foot starts tapping, and her eyebrows twitch.
Then just for a moment she shoots HARRIET a furious glance,
but immediately recovers her usual supercilious calm. Her
attention is once more rivetted on her book. HARRIET laughs,
gets up, and wanders back to CON and MAUD; throws herself
in chair.*)
She rose like a trout to the fly. I asked had she heard
how Mr de Lacey flirted with the youngest Miss Unwin
at the Clareboys' picnic. I told her it was the talk of the
neighbourhood, and every servants' hall for miles round
had it a match.
(*Silence.*)
Really, how dull you are, you –
(*Pause.*)
Con. Are you ill?
CON: Leave me alone.
HARRIET: You're feverish – all scarlet patches. And you
look guilty – what are you up to?
(*MAJOR ROSS-MARTIN mutters incoherently in his sleep.
They glance at him briefly, irritated.*)
You've a secret.
(*CON bends over her work.*)

Why, how scared you look.

(*CON sews wildly.*)

What can it be, I wonder? You've been seeing the
Granvilles against Papa's orders – no? No. You've been
playing whist with the curate in the village hall – no?
No. (*Pause.*) I declare I'm baffled.

(*Sits back.*)

Well. All things considered, I think it can only be – a
lover. There, I've scored. But you haven't told anyone,
have you? Why not? Because Papa would disapprove?
Ah, look at you, how transparent you are –

(*She sits considering.*)

And perhaps you're not sure of the lover either. He
hasn't declared himself.

(*She speaks briskly.*)

Why, I do believe it must be Mr Rudd.

(*CON pricks her finger, cries out.*)

Bullseye.

MAUD: (*Fury.*) Go back to your drawing. Start now –
today –

(*HARRIET looks at her in surprise.*)

It's boredom makes you so cruel. You have nothing but
teasing to amuse you. You'd be so different if you used
your talent – it's God-given, remember. All talent comes
from God. Neglect it at your peril.

CON: Stop it, please – Violet will hear –

(*They all look at VIOLET. Silence.*)

HARRIET: It's a long time since she turned a page.

(*Silence. They watch.*)

Like living in the immediate neighbourhood of Vesuvius,
don't you think? (*Pause.*) Look at her – her antennae are
quivering – searching. Violet knows.

CON: Oh, can no one keep her out of this room tomorow?

HARRIET: Ah. Coming tomorrow, is he?

(*CON looks petrified.*)

So that's it. And you want Violet kept out. I could do it.
Easily. If I wanted to.

CON: How?

HARRIET: No need for you to know.

CON: Ah, Harriet, how good you are –

HARRIET: If I wanted to. I said.

CON: But you will? Won't you?

HARRIET: I don't understand you, Con. You've always been the most fastidious of the lot of us – how can you even consider marrying the little bootman? And there's something odd about him, you know. I don't think you'd have everything your own way –
(*Silence.*)

CON: Keep Violet out of the room tomorrow and Hilary shall have my emeralds for lunch.
(*MAUD looks horrified. VIOLET silently shuts her book. Sits motionless.*)

HARRIET: You mean Barbara. I've told you before, emeralds wouldn't suit Hilary. But you never listen –

MAUD: Harriet! How could you even consider it?

CON: Take them.

HARRIET: Thank you, Con. I will.

MAUD: How can you be so base?
(*VIOLET sits quietly, listening. Puts her book down.*)

CON: Leave her alone. She's going to help me. Harriet never says she can do a thing if she can't –

MAUD: How you've coarsened, Harriet. You used to be so kind – you gave help freely, from your heart.

HARRIET: You don't understand. Why did Aunt Dora leave them to Con? I'm older than she is and I've got two daughters. They should be mine by rights.

MAUD: Rights? No one has rights. Do you want to end up like Violet? Obsessed with wrongs you think were done to you?

HARRIET: I'm not like Violet – not at all.
(*Unnoticed, VIOLET smiles wolfishly.*)
And I haven't coarsened – have I? Surely not –

MAUD: If you take Con's emeralds for helping save her life God may forgive you, but I won't.

CON: Leave her alone, Maud. It's between her and me – a nursery bargain, like we've always had. Why, you took my most precious book in return for your musical box –

HARRIET: And I used to give Con trinkets to keep out of the way when Toby came – just like we're doing now –

(*Slowly VIOLET gets up; stands. The others are too involved to notice.*)

MAUD: No. It is not.

CON: It's between Harriet and me, so please keep out of it. Just like you to make a fuss about a nursery game.

HARRIET: Anyone would think we'd done something dreadful, the pair of us.

(*Slowly, VIOLET starts towards them.*)

MAUD: Not the pair of you. Only you, Harriet. If you take those emeralds you will be diminished for the rest of your life.

(*Silence.*)

It's an irretrievable step. Don't take it. Give yourself the chance to live at peace with your conscience.

HARRIET: (*Fury.*) It's so unfair, you bring everything back to God, make a mountain out of a molehill – why can't you let small things stay small? Why –

(*MAUD looks at her.*)

Oh, all right, then, all right –

(*MAUD looks at her with vast relief.*)

(*Snarls.*) Heaven preserve me from the good –

CON: Harriet, don't listen to her – stop interfering, Maud, you know I need her help –

HARRIET: Be quiet, Con, drat you. You shall have it.

(*MAJOR ROSS-MARTIN twitches in his sleep.*)

MAJOR ROSS-MARTIN: Their eyes – their eyes – why do they look so – so –

(*CON is overcome by a fit of coughing; MAUD goes to her anxiously. Unnoticed, VIOLET is now right behind them, very near. She stands, silent, unnoticed.*)

CON: Oh, leave me alone – you make me worse, if you
didn't fuss I'd be perfectly all right –

MAUD: You can tell that to Doctor Greene. He'll be here
early tomorrow morning.

CON: (*Fretful.*) Silly man, why does he keep coming? He
does me no good – he looks so gloomy and depresses
me so – it's bad for me to be depressed –
(*CON coughs again, attack more prolonged. Both MAUD and
HARRIET are bending over her; she is holding her handkerchief to her mouth. All three jump as VIOLET speaks,
then gaze at her, motionless.*)

VIOLET: Blood on your handkerchief, Constance?
(*They all look at her, paralysed.*)
I shall speak to Doctor Greene myself.

MAUD: Don't, Violet –

VIOLET: It's my duty. You don't seem to realise what a
serious risk of infection we run, all of us. And you know
how the idea of illness upsets Mama. I'll certainly tell
Doctor Greene to insist on Constance staying in bed
tomorrow.

CON: No, Violet – please, please –

VIOLET: Why Constance – you're trembling.
(*Silence. She stands motionless, watching CON.*)
Really, the slightest thing upsets you. It's because you're
so weak, you see. A day in bed will do you all the good
in the world. And there's nothing special about
tomorrow, is there? (*Pause.*) Just another day, like all the
rest.
(*VIOLET walks swiftly back to her chair. HARRIET makes
a furious gesture and knocks a pile of books off a table and
onto the floor. MAJOR ROSS-MARTIN wakes up shouting,
and they all freeze, almost crouch.*)

MAJOR ROSS-MARTIN: No more soup – of course there's
more soup, they're dying, look, dying – no more soup
when they're dying – starving – starving – Seamus –
look at his eyes – tell him to stop looking at me –

Seamus, shut your eyes – what have I done you should look at me like that? I can't watch – I can't –
(*He starts from sleep, a look of horror on his face which gradually dies. He glares round the room, shaking his head from side to side.*)
Well? Why aren't you singing? Why the devil aren't you singing? Daughters, ugh – daughters – nothing but a damned expense. At least you can sing – sing for your supper – come on, come on – Constance –
(*CON walks reluctantly over to the piano; sits down, strikes a few chords; suddenly strikes the piano as though it was a harp and starts singing.*)

CON: 'When I am laid, am laid in earth – remember me – remember me –'
(*The effect is shattering, even on VIOLET; whatever song they expected it wasn't this.*)

MAJOR ROSS-MARTIN: Stop!
(*CON stops. MRS ROSS-MARTIN stops rocking.*)

MRS ROSS-MARTIN: Not – that's not – not a nice song –

MAJOR ROSS-MARTIN: You've upset your mother.

MRS ROSS-MARTIN: – not a nice song –

MAJOR ROSS-MARTIN: I won't have it, do you hear?
Keep all – that – out of your mother's drawing room – I want a song fit for gentlewomen. Come on – Violet – Maud – Harriet – come on, I say –
(*Each rises in turn.*)
Daughters, ugh – daughters – sing out now – 'Believe me if all those endearing young charms' – sing up, sing up –
(*He recomposes himself for sleep, MRS ROSS-MARTIN goes back to rocking, while CON plays, and they all sing, looking simply furious, from 'Believe me' down to 'The same look that she gave when he rose'.*)
Stop! That *morceau* again – 'Oh, the heart' – come on, come on!
(*They sing it again.*)
Again!

(*They begin again, but CON starts coughing. MAUD and HARRIET look at her anxiously. The coughing gets worse, she has to stop playing. The voices of the others quaver and die.*)

THREE

The same room, the next morning. MAUD is tidying an over-flowing workbox; CON is almost dancing about the room.

CON: Dear Doctor Greene! Delightful Doctor Greene! How can I ever have thought him gloomy? 'There's no need for Miss Constance to stay in bed if she doesn't choose.' Oh, Violet's face – dear man, what a spoke he put in her wheel. And Harriet, good, kind Harriet, will finish her off –
(MAUD doesn't look up from tidying; speaks with unexpected savagery.)
MAUD: How can you leave your work-box in this state? Have you no pride?
(CON gazes at her, shocked.)
Look at it. The lid won't even shut. And look, there's your book lying on the floor for someone else to pick up – why do you never think about other people?
(MAUD picks up book, tidies it away.)
Oh, it's not your fault, it's mine. I've always spoilt you, so of course you've no consideration –
(She sees CON's shocked face. Silence.)
I'm sorry. I was upset – just for the moment –
CON: You're never cross. What's the matter?
MAUD: I'm sorry, sorry. I didn't mean anything. I've a bit of a headache.
CON: You never have headaches. *(Laughs.)* It's you need Doctor Greene, not me.
(MAUD turns back to box.)
MAUD: There. At least the lid shuts now.
CON: What's the time?
MAUD: Oh, Con, not again –
CON: What's the time, what's the time?
MAUD: Twenty minutes to eleven.

(*She starts going round the room tidying, plumping up cushions.*)

CON: How can I wait for twenty minutes? Suppose he can't get the words out? Will we discuss the weather first? Oh, this is the worst moment of my life. Am I tidy?

(*She tries to see her reflection in the glass of the dead pheasant painting. Can't. Rushes to MAUD.*)

How do I look, Maud? How do I look?

(*MAUD stands silent, looking at her.*)

Well?

MAUD: Wild. Desperate. Yourself.

(*She turns away abruptly and starts plumping up cushions.*)

CON: Leave those cushions alone, do –

MAUD: We can't live in a pig-sty.

CON: Why not? It would be warm. And friendly. (*Pause.*) What's the time?

MAUD: Where's your watch?

CON: Broken.

MAUD: (*Sudden irritation.*) You see? You take no care of your things, you –

(*She pulls herself together.*)

Don't take any notice, it's this silly headache.

(*Looks at her watch.*)

Eighteen minutes to eleven.

(*She goes back to tidying. CON rushes and confronts her.*)

CON: Will you stop tidying?

MAUD: Sit down. Be still. Or you'll start coughing.

CON: Then sit with me –

(*Pulls MAUD down onto sofa.*)

I want my thoughts to move slowly like summer clouds –

(*MAUD takes out her workbox, starts sewing.*)

Eighteen minutes. How am I to fill up eighteen minutes?

(*MAUD answers without much hope.*)

MAUD: Read a book?

CON: Are you mad? I couldn't see the print. How pale
    your emotions must be if you think I could sit down now
    and read –

MAUD: Not pale. Ordered. Under control.

CON: I could recite the Kings of England. I suppose. Well.
    Who came first? (*Pause.*) Alfred. Ethelred – no, that's
    wrong. (*Pause.*) I'll begin at 1066. William the
    Conqueror. William Rufus. Henry I. (*Pause.*) Bit of a
    blank after Henry I. Once you get to the Georges, of
    course, you're home and dried – four of 'em, all in a row.
    And those Charleses – how do they fit in? (*Pause.*) Maud.
    Who comes after Henry I? No, don't tell me, I don't
    care, what do I care for all the Kings of England,
    ridiculous kings, why should they expect me to know
    their names? Let 'em go hang – what's the time?
    (*MAUD looks at her.*)
    Ah, just this once, Maud, dearest Maud –

MAUD: Sixteen and a half minutes to eleven.

CON: Sixteen – what nonsense. I can't have forgotten the
    complete list of the Kings of England in ninety seconds,
    think what you're saying, Maud.
    (*Silence. MAUD works; CON sits kicking her feet about.*
    Several times opens her mouth to speak; doesn't. Then turns
    to MAUD in a rush. Sits forward, opens her mouth to speak.)

MAUD: Fifteen and a half.

CON: Well, that's progress. I suppose. Fifteen and a half
    minutes can't last for ever. Or perhaps they can. Perhaps
    time's stopped and I'm stuck for ever waiting for Mr
    Rudd and forgetting the kings of England and getting
    more and more desperate as time doesn't pass –
    (*She gets up and walks up and down the room. Stops suddenly.*)
    Why is waiting for Mr Rudd so nerve-racking when I
    don't give two straws for him? Look at the state I'm in –
    trembling, can't think properly – anyone would think I
    was in love with the man. This is how people in love
    behave, isn't it? Or so we're led to believe. Don't know
    much about it, do we? Not in this house.

(*Throws herself into chair.*)
The novels I read are full of it. And no one in the songs
Papa makes us sing can think of anything else.
(*Sings.*) 'Have you ever been in love, my boys
And have you felt the pain?
I'd rather be in gaol, my sons,
Than be in love again –'
And so on and so on. And so on. Clearly there's a lot of
it about. Do you suppose there's any in the village?

MAUD: (*Suddenly upset.*) Do stop talking!
(*CON looks at her in bewilderment.*)

CON: I was trying to be company for myself –
(*Goes to MAUD, hugs her.*)
Maud! What's wrong with you? Don't you want me to
get away and stay alive?
(*MAUD embraces her. They stand.*)

MAUD: I wish you everything in the world, my darling.

CON: Oh, Maud. What am I doing? Do I really think life
with him is worth struggling for? Suppose I marry Mr
Rudd and Rutland Gate and then one day I fall in love? I
could, you know.
(*She clutches MAUD.*)
Help me – I've lost my nerve. If I settle for Mr Rudd,
the Furies will pursue me. I'll be living in Rutland Gate,
going to At Homes and concerts, a comfortable matron,
then one day, as I get into my carriage, I'll turn my head
and see my Waterloo.

MAUD: What on earth are you talking about?

CON: The man who's out there somewhere. Waiting.

MAUD: I knew someone should vet those novels you read.

CON: It's not if, but when. He'll come, all right, oh, yes.
And I'll be done for – my heart and my peace and my
soul – all lost.
(*Silence.*)

MAUD: I don't think you need worry, my darling.
(*CON goes over to fireplace, takes down white porcelain figure
of a cupid.*)

CON: Look at this Cupid, Maud. He's warning us. There he
stands, finger to his lips, looking so douce.
(*She reads the inscription.*)
'*Qui que tu sois, voici ton maître*
Il est – le fut – ou le doit être.'
Whoever you are, here is your master. Was your master
Or is. If neither – beware tomorrow.

MAUD: How lucky Mademoiselle Hortense is no longer
with us to hear such a slipshod and inaccurate
translation.
(*CON holds Cupid in front of MAUD's face.*)

CON: Look at him, Maud. He's warning us about love –
well, not love, it's a far cry from your gentle Jesus –
(*MAUD looks smitten.*)
– passion, that's the word. Passion is out there, lying in
wait. Sees his moment and he's on you, a spider with a
poor gasping fly. No escape. Could even happen to you,
you know. You're not immune, so don't you think it. One
day you, even you, may find yourself panting, breathless
– out of control, Maud. Totally out of control. And what
will you do then, poor thing? Pray to your Heavenly
Bridegroom to protect you?

MAUD: Con!

CON: Ah, Maud, dear Maud, I didn't mean it, I didn't mean
it, I'm sorry, sorry, sorry –
(*She embraces MAUD.*)
But what am I to do, what am I to do? I must decide
before he comes –
(*She goes to vase of dahlias on piano, takes one.*)
We used to play with daisies, remember? He loves me –
he loves me not –
(*She drops one petal on the floor.*)
Life – but with Mr Rudd –

MAUD: Oh, Con, not all over the floor –

CON: – or –
(*She drops another petal.*)
Death.

(Drops them one by one as she speaks.
MAUD is her knees, picking them up. Several of them fall on
her head.)
Life. Death. Life. Death. Life.
(She goes faster and faster, saying the words under her breath.
Looks at the last petal.)
Death. The petals say death.
(She drops it.)

MAUD: No wonder Hilda gets cross –
(CON stands motionless.)

CON: *(Shouts.)* No! Who cares about the silly petals – they
don't know what they're talking about – I'm going to
live. Do you hear, Maud? I'm going to live for ever –

MAUD: Stop it!

CON: Waterloo! Come out of the shadows! I know you're
there –

MAUD: Con, Con – listen – I must tell you –
(The door opens and VIOLET comes in. There is an immediate
hush and chill; CON looks petrified, clutches MAUD, shouts.)

CON: No!

VIOLET: Flowers in your hair, Maud. How quaint.

CON: What are you doing here?

VIOLET: Why, I've come to read my book. I hope to finish
it before luncheon.

CON: Where's Harriet? Why isn't she here?

VIOLET: Barbara had a fall. Harriet is doing her duty for
once and attending to her.
(CON sits down with a thump.)
Goodness, Constance. Your best dress. What a special
day it must be –
(CON gazes at her, all hope gone.)
In the morning, too. You're making quite a guy of
yourself, aren't you? Quite a figure of fun.
(MAUD puts an arm round CON.)
Or perhaps you're expecting someone?
(Silence.)

It must be someone very grand to merit your best dress.
Why didn't you warn the rest of us so we could all
dazzle together?

CON: (*To MAUD.*) Oh where is Harriet?

VIOLET: (*To MAUD.*) What made you think dahlia petals
were becoming?

CON: Find her, Maud – quickly –

VIOLET: Whatever Doctor Greene says, you have a very
hectic flush, Constance. You know how frightened Mama
is of infection.

(*The door opens; HARRIET comes in; CON rushes to her.*)

CON: Ah, where's your promise, then?

HARRIET: I'm here, aren't I?

CON: Look – look at her squatting there –
(*Shouts at VIOLET.*)
You – you malevolent incubus –

HARRIET: I couldn't leave Barbara with that stupid Jenny.
But I'm here now. Leave Violet to me. It won't take long.
(*CON and MAUD stand as though paralysed.*)
Go on –
(*CON grabs MAUD.*)

CON: Come along, do, didn't you hear? Don't dawdle so –

VIOLET: You'll have a chance to tidy yourself, Maud.
Petals in your hair may have looked sweet when you
were a child, but you're rather past it, don't you think?
(*CON hustles MAUD out, shutting the door behind them.
HARRIET looks at VIOLET, who sits, eyes downcast.*)

HARRIET: Mr Rudd is Con's one chance of staying alive.

VIOLET: She should be in bed, not breathing germs over
the rest of us.

HARRIET: If you stop him proposing and she dies, you'll
have killed her.
(*VIOLET shrugs, picks up a book.*)
But of course you mean to sit here and give him no
chance.

VIOLET: I have no intention of being driven from the
drawing-room by Mr Rudd. Why should I?

HARRIET: Why, indeed?

(*VIOLET opens her book and starts reading. HARRIET sits and looks at VIOLET, as though examining a strange animal. VIOLET goes on reading.*)

You always get your own way, don't you?

(*VIOLET half smiles to herself; turns a page.*)

But not this time.

(*VIOLET puts her book down, looks at HARRIET. Silence.*)

A few years ago whisky started disappearing at a terrible rate. It had always – well, leaked a bit – but now it was beyond a joke. So Maud was on the point of sacking John, who was the obvious culprit. But you stood up for him, I remember. Made her change her mind.

VIOLET: John's been with us a long time. He deserved support.

HARRIET: I agree. And with an old servant you can hardly call it stealing. More like taking a little help to lighten the load through the long hard day.

VIOLET: I felt that to be the case, certainly.

HARRIET: You were quite impassioned on his behalf.

VIOLET: We owed him help. Consideration.

HARRIET: Indeed we did. And do. (*Pause.*) But it doesn't ring true, does it? You? Show consideration for an old servant? You? Take a humane view? Never in life, my dear. Never in life.

(*She sits back, looks at VIOLET.*)

So I set out to find the cause of your unwonted generosity of spirit.

(*Pause.*)

It didn't take long. It's not John who takes the whisky. It's you.

(*VIOLET stiffens. Silence.*)

Oh, he helps himself, of course he does, but quite moderately, all things considered.

(*Silence. VIOLET is rigid.*)

It began a long time ago, didn't it? Probably soon after Aunt Emma died, and with her your vaunted future. Oh,

I don't expect you to confide in me. If ever there was a
chance we might have been close, it's too late now –

VIOLET: (*Fury.*) Now! Why –

(*She stops. Hisses at HARRIET.*)

You cuckoo – you cuckoo in the nest.

(*Silence. HARRIET looks at her in amazement.*)

Oh, don't pretend you don't know what I'm talking
about. Too late now? It's been too late since the day you
were born.

HARRIET: (*Astonished.*) What?

VIOLET: You stole Mama from me – and Maud – you stole
them both with your beguiling deceitful ways. Until you
were born Mama played with me in the evenings, read to
me – how I looked forward to my time with her, I
thought about it all day long. Until you were born and
stole her heart away. She had no time for me ever again.
Of course you knew what you were doing – don't dare
pretend you didn't.

HARRIET: On my word, Violet, I had no idea. I knew you
didn't like me, but you didn't like anyone – always on
your own – (*Pause.*) Well I'm blowed – Maud was right.

(*She sits, staring at VIOLET.*)

She said you'd never got over me being born. And I
thought it was just one of her silly ideas. Good heavens.
Maud was right.

(*She gets up, stares at VIOLET.*)

So if it hadn't been for me, you'd have been – what? Full
of the milk of human kindness? A little ray of sunshine?
In any case, quite human. Well, that's your story. But I
find it hard to believe. Because I remember you from my
earliest days as you are now – someone who couldn't
brook competition, who enjoyed giving pain. Your
cutting tongue has been with me always.

(*VIOLET shoots a furious look at her; speaks in a voice that
is not her own.*)

VIOLET: What are you going to do?

HARRIET: You were born what you are now. I can't remember you ever rejoicing, or crying, with the rest of us. Not once. You weren't rejected, you rejected us. You were always apart.

VIOLET: Enough of that. Answer me. What are you going to do?

(*HARRIET is gazing at VIOLET, fascinated.*)

HARRIET: Mm? Oh, yes, of course. The whisky. Well. I've known for years and done nothing. As far as I'm concerned you can go on burying empty bottles in Foel Wood for the rest of your life. If you leave Con alone with her little boot man.

VIOLET: And if I don't?

HARRIET: I shall tell. Of course. (*Pause.*) I can't imagine what Papa will do – keep you permanently locked in your room, do you think? What shouting there'll be, what roaring. But the point is your source of supply will be cut off. And of course you could never buy the stuff – you're like the rest of us, you've no money, not two pennies to rub together. Oh, the shifts we're put to, all four of us –

(*Silence.*)

You'll leave Con alone.

VIOLET: Yes.

(*She gets up, prepares to go.*)

HARRIET: By the way, that bracelet you're wearing –

(*VIOLET stops on her way to the door.*)

I think Barbara would like it when she's older. But perhaps I'd better take it now, you might forget.

(*Slowly VIOLET takes off her bracelet and hands it over. HARRIET examines it.*)

Two stones missing, how rough you are on your jewellery. As rough as you are on people. Perhaps you shouldn't have any. Perhaps I should have –

(*Pause. HARRIET swings the bracelet in one hand. Looks at it. Suddenly shudders.*)

No. Take it –

(*She throws it at VIOLET, who picks it up.*)

I was wrong. I – I don't want it.

(*VIOLET goes towards the door.*)

I've never liked you. You were odious in the nursery and you've been odious ever since. You may pretend to yourself it's my fault, but whatever the reason, you are what you are, and that's that. You have to put up with it and so do we. (*Pause.*) But I'm sorry you're in hell.

(*VIOLET turns swiftly.*)

VIOLET: Where you'll be joining me. Soon enough.

(*She confronts HARRIET.*)

How did your precious Toby die?

(*Silence.*)

HARRIET: Pneumonia –

VIOLET: Pneumonia.

(*Silence.*)

HARRIET: Yes.

VIOLET: He died of drink.

(*Silence.*)

HARRIET: He died of drink.

VIOLET: And your father is drunk every evening. And your sister drinks. Do you imagine your children will escape? It's already clear one of them hasn't. Ulick is done for.

HARRIET: Ulick! He's only eight –

VIOLET: Sometimes Papa gives him a sip of sherry. Only sometimes. So Ulick is never sure whether it's coming his way or not. The next time it happens, watch the anxiety in his face – his expression as he sits waiting on the edge of his chair. I recognise that expression, of course I do. Because it's my own. Because your precious Ulick and I are two of a kind. Oh, you'll have to watch him. And you will. Now I've warned you you'll never stop watching. From now on your days and your nights will be haunted. The suspicion will poison your life.

HARRIET: There speaks the little ray of sunshine, the milk of human kindness coursing through her veins. No, Violet. You were never like the rest of us.

VIOLET: I may be, as you so picturesquely put it, in hell. But as you will be joining me I'll have company, won't I?

(*VIOLET goes out swiftly. Almost at once CON rushes in, followed by MAUD. HARRIET stands frowning, lost in thought.*)

CON: How did you do it? Oh, clever, clever Harriet, I'll love you for ever –

HARRIET: (*To herself.*) But he's only eight –

CON: What did you do to Violet? What did you say?

HARRIET: (*Focuses.*) You can entertain the little bootman undisturbed. Papa is out shooting, Mama is in her private world, Violet's upstairs. I will stay in the nursery. (*She starts towards the door; turns.*)

Take what you want, said God. Take it and pay. You'll get what you want, Con. I wonder what the payment will be. And whether it will be worth it.

(*She goes out. CON and MAUD stand for a minute, then CON begins singing, to the tune of Rory O'More, and doing a jig, slowly at first, then faster and faster, sweeping MAUD, protesting, along with her, so that they are both doing a wild and over-excited dance.*)

CON: 'Papa is out shooting and Violet's upstairs
Mama has gone into her own private world
Papa is out shooting and Violet's upstairs,
And the best of my life is beginning today –'

(*They have not heard John open the door and announce MR RUDD, who now stands silently in the door watching as they stand panting, looking at him, hot and dishevelled. He is not at all like the sisters' picture of him. They have never really looked at him, and have mistaken social embarrassment for genuine diffidence and timidity, of which he has none. In his own world, he is both ruthless and implacable. He is not tall, but he is compact and formidable; looks older than his thirty-*)

five years. His eyes are watchful and his mouth is thin. His clothes are unbecoming and stiff, and add to the illusion of shyness. MAUD and CON gaze at him, and do not take their eyes off him as they speak.)

MAUD: I must go and get the dahlia petals out of my hair.

CON: You got them out. Just now.

MAUD: So I did. If you'll excuse me, Mr Rudd, I must have a word with Annie about luncheon.

CON: Cold lamb stewed fruit and custard.

(MAUD looks at her, frowning. CON still looks at MR RUDD.)

What we're having. No reason to consult Annie.

MAUD: I must do the flowers for the church.

CON: It's Monday, Maud. Do stop making excuses to – to go.

MAUD: All right, I will. I'll go because I feel like it.

(MAUD starts to go; CON makes a grab at her but misses.)

You'll excuse me, Mr Rudd, I have rather a lot to attend to.

(She goes, shutting the door behind her.)

MR RUDD: Please don't be alarmed, Miss Con –

CON: Good heavens, Mr Rudd, why should I be? Do sit down.

(They both sit gingerly upright on the edge of chairs. Silence.)

MR RUDD: I was admiring your ilex avenue on my way here –

CON: It's considered very fine.

MR RUDD: Yes – yes, I thought it was – was –

(He frowns, pauses.)

CON: Fine?

MR RUDD: Yes. Fine.

CON: People often admire it.

MR RUDD: I'm sure they do.

CON: Apparently no one knows where you'd find a finer avenue –

MR RUDD: No doubt.

CON: Of ilexes, I mean.

MR RUDD: Ilexes, yes.
(*Silence.*)
I expect you know a lot about ilexes.
CON: Nothing at all.
MR RUDD: Oh. I thought you might be an authority. As your avenue is so fine.
CON: But I'm not.
MR RUDD: No.
CON: I only know they're uncommon. Especially for Wales.
(*MR RUDD has an attack of coughing; speaks through it.*)
MR RUDD: You certainly don't see many ilexes in Wales –
CON: What?
MR RUDD: I said 'you certainly don't see many ilexes in Wales'.
CON: Oh. I didn't hear. You were coughing, you see.
MR RUDD: So I was.
(*Silence.*)
CON: Of course we have rhododendrums too. Like everyone else.
MR RUDD: Of course.
CON: Very pretty when they're in flower.
MR RUDD: Oh, very.
CON: When they're not in flower, of course, they're not so pretty. Just green.
(*Silence. MR RUDD shuffles. CON sighs.*)
I always say there's too much green in the country. My sister Violet wears a lot of green. Such a mistake. And purple, she looks like a rhododendrum that's reverted to type. They do that, you know. they all go the same boring purple. Then they're not pretty at all. Just common.
MR RUDD: No one could call your ilex avenue common.
CON: Common! Our avenue? No, indeed. Why on earth should they? Really, Mr Rudd, what a suggestion.
MR RUDD: (*Stammering.*) Oh, Miss Con, really, I didn't mean – of course I didn't mean – your avenue common, no, indeed – never – I didn't mean –

(*His voice dies away. He wipes his forehead.*)

CON: When this rigmarole is over, Mr Rudd, are you going to propose?

(*Silence.*)

MR RUDD: You know I am.

CON: I've been angling for you. For weeks I've thought of nothing but how to bring you to book. What an ugly phrase, Mr Rudd. An ugly phrase for an ugly wish. I didn't realise when it came to the point I would feel so shabby and mean. I only wanted to marry you to escape and stay alive. I'm ill, you see.

MR RUDD: I know.

CON: So I tried to cheat you.

MR RUDD: I know that too. (*Pause.*) I'll marry you on any terms.

(*CON looks at him in amazement.*)

Try me. Make your terms.

CON: Why?

MR RUDD: Because of the way you move. The glance from your eyes –

CON: Is that all?

MR RUDD: What else is there?

CON: (*Amazement.*) Good heavens. Am I your Waterloo?

MR RUDD: If you mean what I take you to – (*Snarls.*) Yes.

CON: Then of course I can't marry you. I've never met mine. But he's out there. I don't know what's kept him, must be hanging about in limbo somewhere. But suppose I married you and then he came bursting out of his limbo bold as brass?

MR RUDD: I'll risk it.

CON: You're much more dashing than any of us had noticed. And brave. (*Pause.*) I like you.

MR RUDD: Marry me.

CON: Didn't you hear me say I like you? How can I? We've agreed there's only one reason for marrying.

MR RUDD: Most people would consider the reasons for
which you planned to accept me more than adequate. As
it's you, so do I.

CON: What does it matter what most people would think if
we know it's a sham from the word go?

MR RUDD: I want you on any terms.

CON: If I accepted it would be purely to stay alive.

MR RUDD: Any terms.

CON: I shan't change. I shan't wake one morning and say
Good Heavens, Mr Rudd was my Waterloo all along and
I never noticed.

MR RUDD: Any terms.

CON: You're leaving me no choice.

MR RUDD: I mean to leave you none. Nor do I intend to
give you any time. You must come with me now.
(*CON gasps in astonishment.*)
In view of your father's views on blood, Miss Con – and
I'm well aware he'd prefer me to use the tradesman's
entrance – you cannot imagine he would welcome me as
a son-in-law.

CON: How cogently you put things – why did none of us
ever notice you?

MR RUDD: Because you are all a great deal noisier than I
am. Noticing other people – listening to them – is not
your strong point. You spend your time shouting at each
other, visitors can barely make themselves heard. But I
can assure you I am not negligible.

CON: So I see.
(*Silence.*)
(*Flustered.*) I may not be suitable for you –

MR RUDD: You're not.

CON: Oh.

MR RUDD: I should vastly prefer a sensible young woman
with none of your terrifying frivolity. And you're useless.
You couldn't cook my breakfast or darn my clothes.
You've no sense. But you've put a spell on me, on my
eyes and my heart, so if the countryside was littered with

suitable young women, I couldn't see them. I can only see you. I was finished the moment I saw you.

CON: So Waterloo unhinges the mind.

MR RUDD: (*Fury.*) When I think how useless you are and how low you rate me – why, old Leggatt of Northampton would give his eyes to snare me for his daughter – and give her a settlement would buy up half the county – when I think of my reputation at home and the way everyone jumps to do my orders –

(*He goes right up to her.*)

– and then I think of you and your feckless family and the way you condescend to me, I tell, you, I'm half mad. Why, you can't even pay your laundry bills. But it doesn't stop you using the laundry, oh, no. Some poor devil of an honest tradesman can go bankrupt because of you, but it would never occur to you to turn to and learn to wash your own things. There'd be some excuse if you were stupid, but you're not. You're clever, the whole pack of you – even your father – clever as a barrel-load of monkeys. (*Yells.*) And a fat lot of good it's done you –

(*With great difficulty he gets a grip on himself.*)

When I leave this house you're coming with me. I have an Aunt in Shrewsbury who has offered to have you to stay while I make arrangements for the wedding.

CON: How could I have thought you negligible?

MR RUDD: You didn't look. But I can assure you, you're marrying someone who can protect his interests from any poaching stranger. I can smell danger when it's there, and deceit and treachery. I'll guard what's mine.

CON: What an odd way to think.

MR RUDD: It's a tradesman's way. You'll find it strange after this feckless household, but you'll get used to it. I look after what's my own.

(*Silence.*)

CON: (*Urgent.*) You'll take me to the sun?

MR RUDD: Isn't that the point? (*Pause.*) We'll honeymoon in Italy.

CON: Honeymoon – how – (*Pause.*) I'll come.

MR RUDD: Of course you will. You're not a fool, you want to stay alive. Go and tell your sister.

(*They look at each other. CON makes for the door; goes. MR RUDD, left alone, wanders round the room, clearly despising it. Stops in front of the Cupid. Picks it up, examines it for some time, standing stock still. Puts it down.*)

MR RUDD: Tchah.

(*He goes on wandering round the room, but keeps looking back at the Cupid. Suddenly addresses it, savagely.*)

I've got her. She'll be my wife under my roof. And that's all there is to it. (*Pause.*) Yes. All there is to it.

(*Makes another irritated noise, turns his back on Cupid. MAUD comes in, followed by CON and HARRIET.*)

MAUD: Oh, look after her, Mr Rudd, look after her – she's so delicate –

MR RUDD: It's arranged. And I've got the special licence – we can be married in three days.

HARRIET: (*Aside to CON.*) So you brought him to book.

CON: (*Passion.*) It wasn't like that – it wasn't like that at all –

MAUD: No time to buy wedding clothes, oh dear – it's so awkward – and Papa – who's to tell –

CON: No one. Mr Rudd and I leave now. You say I'm in bed with a temperature, you bring my food up yourself and don't let anyone in – really, it's too easy, Maud, don't make complications –

(*MAUD looks distraught.*)

Well, of course, if you feel you can't do it there's the end of it. I'll just stay here and die.

MAUD: I didn't say I wouldn't, but –

CON: Maud, you're an angel, the only nice one of the four of us – it'll be the easiest thing in the world, you'll see. Oh, how Papa will create when he finds out – think of the roaring went on the other day – and only because his sardine dish got broken, ugly old thing it was, too –

MR RUDD: We can't stop here gossiping all day, Miss Con.

CON: Of course we can't – Maud, you mustn't keep us here any longer, chattering away – where's my novel?

MAUD: Really, Con – this isn't the time –

CON: (*Surprised.*) But I'm only half way through it.

(*MR RUDD is looking grim and formidable. He is certainly not smiling indulgently. MAUD picks up book from the sofa, hands it to CON.*)

Oh, thank you, Maud – really I think you'd better come too – you always find everything for me –

MAUD: Be off with you now, Con –

CON: Oh – my cloak –

HARRIET: I'll get it –

(*HARRIET goes out.*)

CON: I'm always losing things, Mr Rudd. Will you find them for me?

MR RUDD: (*Grim.*) You'll have to wait and see.

(*CON looks at him, disconcerted. HARRIET comes back, carrying cloak.*)

HARRIET: It's torn. You can't elope in a torn cloak.

(*MAUD takes it at once, goes to her work-box, finds her needle.*)

MR RUDD: Miss Con will have plenty of time to mend it when she's with my aunt.

CON: Oh, I'm hopeless at mending things – Hilda does it for me. And Maud, of course –

MAUD: It only needs a stitch.

MR RUDD: You'll have to learn. What would my aunt say if I told her you couldn't mend your own cloak?

CON: Will your Aunt like me?

MR RUDD: Probably not. She's had a hard life.

CON: Oh. I'm sorry.

MR RUDD: She's not funny, if that's what you were hoping. But being funny isn't everything.

CON: (*Unconvinced.*) No – no, of course not –

(*MAUD bites off thread and hands CON her cloak.*)

MAUD: There. It's done. Now, off with you –

HARRIET: Good heavens. The rain's stopped.

CON: And look – the sun's coming out –

HARRIET: (*To herself.*) A miracle. God and Maud at it again.

(*MAUD takes CON's hand, pulls her towards the door.*)

MAUD: Away with you, Con –

CON: No. I want to leave through the French windows – oh, the times I've gazed through them yearning to get away –

(*She throws the French windows open.*)

The sun – how fresh everything smells – but Maud, I'll get my feet wet –

MAUD: Off with you Con. Never mind your feet.

CON: You never let me get my feet wet – why have you stopped fussing?

(*CON and MAUD look at each other.*)

MR RUDD: I'll carry you.

CON: How romantic –

(*She hugs HARRIET, then MAUD, who embraces her with passion, then stands like stone. MR RUDD picks CON up; stands still for a moment looking at her. CON, who was laughing, is suddenly silenced, disconcerted. An ominous moment. Then it is over; he carries her through the French windows. CON shouts back to them.*)

I must wave to Violet – she'll be watching from her bedroom window. She'll be looking out of that window for the rest of her life – while I'm off and away – in Monte Carlo – Venice – the Isles of Greece, the Isles of Greece –

(*MAUD and HARRIET watch in silence as MR RUDD carries CON over the grass, CON waving wildly. When they are nearly out of sight, MAUD shouts.*)

MAUD: Goodbye, my darling – goodbye.

(*They watch them out of sight. MAUD gazes at the spot where they disappeared.*)

How could I? I'll never forgive myself – how could I?

(*HARRIET looks at her, puzzled. MAUD speaks in sudden fury.*)

I was distraught, of course I was, but why, why did I have to –

HARRIET: What are you talking about?

MAUD: It was a disgrace. So untidy you couldn't even shut the lid – oh, but why did –

(*HARRIET looks at her, bewildered.*)

HARRIET: Maud. Are you off your head?

MAUD: Why couldn't I control myself? I always do – you'll bear me out, you know me – I never make a fuss, do I? Oh, Harriet – how could I?

HARRIET: You are off your head.

(*MAUD stands, motionless.*)

MAUD: I snapped at her. Because her work-box was so untidy.

HARRIET: I daresay she deserved it, why are you so upset?

(*Silence.*)

MAUD: Doctor Greene says she'll be dead in three months.

(*Silence.*)

HARRIET: Dear God –

MAUD: He told me this morning. There's no hope. (*Agony.*) And her last memory of me will be how I snapped –

(*HARRIET puts an arm round her. They stand without moving.*)

Should I have told her? I nearly did. But the moment passed and – oh, I don't know. What should I have done? Oh, Harriet, was I right to let her go?

(*They stand by the French windows in silence.*)

HARRIET: Three months. She'll be dead before Christmas.

(*Silence.*)

It doesn't make sense, Maud. It's only yesterday we were children making plans for the future – plans we knew would happen. Where are they, those plans? And where's the future? Where did it go?

MAUD: Con dead.

HARRIET: We'll live out our lives here and die. We will live on in the childrens' memories. Then they will tell their children about the terrible row after Aunt Con ran away. But their children will never be able to sort us out. 'Was it Great Aunt Maud who was the disagreeable one? Was it Great Aunt Violet who was so fond of trees? I can never remember. Anyhow, they've all been dead a long time.'

(*MAUD wanders over to the piano.*)

MAUD: We'll never hear her play again.

(*Very softly she begins to play 'The Kerry Dancing'.*)

HARRIET: And then we'll just be faded photographs, with names on the back that mean nothing to anyone. And one day someone with more sense and less sentimentality than the rest will throw us on the fire. And the last small trace of us will be gone. (*Pause.*) I used to think the world would hold great things for us, when we grew up.

(*She stands by the open window.*)

Toby dead – Con dead before Christmas. What was the point?

MAUD: We'll see them again. In a better world.

(*HARRIET turns to her very swiftly, with violence and passion.*)

HARRIET: Will we? Will we?

(*Jangled chord. MAUD stops playing. Childrens' voices come from the garden.*)

BARBARA: Ulick! Ulick! the rain's stopped – look how the grass sparkles –

HILARY: Race you to the chestnut tree –

ULICK: Let's run for ever.

The End

www.ingramcontent.com/pod-product-compliance
Ingram Content Group UK Ltd.
Pitfield, Milton Keynes, MK11 3LW, UK
UKHW031251020325
455690UK00007B/96